D1604136

J. IRWIN MILLER

J. IRWIN MILLER

THE SHAPING OF AN AMERICAN TOWN

Nancy Kriplen

INDIANA UNIVERSITY PRESS

This book is a publication of

Indiana University Press
Office of Scholarly Publishing
Herman B Wells Library 350
1320 East 10th Street
Bloomington, Indiana 47405 USA

iupress.indiana.edu

The paper used in this publication meets the minimum requirements of the American National Standard for Information Sciences—Permanence of Paper for Printed Library Materials, ANSI Z39.48–1992.

Manufactured in the United States of America

Library of Congress Cataloging-in-Publication Data

Names: Kriplen, Nancy, author.
Title: J. Irwin Miller : the shaping of an American town / Nancy Kriplen.
Description: Bloomington, Indiana : Indiana University Press, 2019. | Includes bibliographical references and index.
Identifiers: LCCN 2018049696 (print) | LCCN 2018050025 (ebook) | ISBN 9780253043825 (e-book) | ISBN 9780253043818 (cl)
Subjects: LCSH: Miller, J. Irwin (Joseph Irwin), 1909-2004. | Industrialists—United States—Biography. | Miller, J. Irwin (Joseph Irwin), 1909-2004—Art patronage. | Midcentury modern (Architecture)—Indiana—Columbus. | Columbus (Ind.)—Biography.
Classification: LCC HC102.5.M467 (ebook) | LCC HC102.5.M467 K75 2019 (print) | DDC 338.7/629250092 [B] —dc23
LC record available at https://lccn.loc.gov/2018049696

1 2 3 4 5 24 23 22 21 20 19

To SAFFRON, LILLY, ELEANOR, CAM, and LUCY

Wouldn't Irwin Miller be great?
He's one of the great people of this world.

—New York City mayor John Lindsay
discussing possible 1968 GOP candidates
for president

Columbus is an improbable town.

—Balthazar Korab, *Columbus Indiana:
An American Landmark*

CONTENTS

ACKNOWLEDGMENTS

FIRST OF ALL, MY THANKS TO MARGARET, CATHERINE, Betsey, Hugh, and Will Miller, the five children of Xenia and Irwin Miller. They put up with my questions about everything from violins to civil rights marches. And they stood back when I'm sure they wanted to jump forward and say, "Wait—do you really understand our family's story?" This book, though it had the family's cooperation, was an independent project.

Research trips are particularly pleasant when friends provide hospitality, as did hosts Maggie Thomas Newsom in Columbus; Shirley Mueller in New York; and Debby Applegate and Bruce Tulgan in New Haven and environs, along with luncheon hostess Catherine Miller. Will Miller provided a splendid tour of the Miller homes at Lake Rosseau in Canada's Muskoka area in a trip funded by a generous grant from the Indiana Arts Commission.

My special thanks to dear Columbus friends Sukey Nie and Maggie Newsom, who cheered me on at the beginning, even though, alas, neither could be present at the finish line. Good friends Jean Glick and Bill and Mary Ann Kendall were of great help because they knew the territory. Sarla Kalsi was always gracious about my questions, and the late Harry McCawley provided more assistance than he realized. Erin Hawkins of the Columbus Visitors Center has been particularly helpful, both in the writing of this book and for an earlier 2013 article for the *New York Times*.

Alyssa Kriplen of MAKwork and Dan Courier of Ram Management helped find and prepare images for this book so that even readers who have never been to Columbus could understand what all the fuss is about. Tom Mason's careful reading kept me from many embarrassing mistakes.

My thanks also to many institutions and their staffs: Art Institute of Chicago Ryerson and Burnham Libraries (Autumn L. Mather), Bartholomew County History Center (Cody Harbaugh), Bartholomew County Public Library (Beth Booth Poor), Christian Theological Seminary (Scott Seay and Don Haymes), Columbia University Center for Oral History (Erica Fugger), Columbus Architectural Archives (Tricia Gilson and Rhonda Bolner), Columbus Clerk Treasurer's Office (Natalie Berkenstock), Columbus Visitors Center (Erin Hawkins, Don Nissen), Cummins Inc. (Katie Zarich and Kelley Creveling), First Christian Church (Maxine Wheeler), First Presbyterian Church (Felipe Martinez), Heritage Columbus (Tracy Souza), Indiana Arts Commission (Sarah Fronczek), Indiana Historical Society William H. Smith Memorial Library (Suzanne Hahn, Nadia Kousari, Susan Sutton, Barbara Quigley, and especially Maire Gurevitz), Indiana Landmarks (Tina Connor, David Frederick, Sam Burgess, and Mark Dollase), Indiana University Library (Erica Dowell and Lou Malcomb), Indianapolis Museum of Art (Bradley Brooks, Alba Fernandez-Keys, and Shelley Selim), Indiana State Library (Justin Davis), Landmark Columbus (Richard McCoy and Brooke Hawkins), LBJ Library (Barbara Cline), Library of Congress (Karen Fishman), Lilly Library–IU Bloomington (Erika Dowell), North Christian Church (Tonya M. Gerardy and Trudi Ellison-Kendall), The Taft School (Christine Afiouni), Yale University Manuscripts and Archives (Suzanne Noruschat and Eric Sonnenberg), and the blog 52 *Weeks of Columbus, Indiana* (Ricky Berkey).

My thanks also to Nancy Baxter, Tom Beczkiewicz, Jill Cashen, Betty Boyd Caroli, George Charbonneau, Bill Cohrs, Nancy

Callaway Fyffe, William S. Gardiner, David Goodrich, Lee Hamilton, Jim Henderson, Bob Holden, Owen Hungerford, Jim Joseph, Christian M. Korab, Glen Kwok, Gerry LaFollette, Cho-Liang (Jimmy) Lin, Beth Lowe, Bob Lowe, Claudia Stevens Maddox, Marvin Mass, John Mutz, Jonathan Nesci, Natalie Olinger, John Pickett, Diane Richards, Steve Risting, Cynthia Cline Roberts, Kevin Roche, Michelangelo Sabatino, Henry Schacht, David Sechrest, Lauren Smythe, Joe Stevenson, Frank Thomas, Daly Walker, Fay Williams, Marianne Wokeck, and Dan Yates.

Agent Roger Williams of New England Publishing Associates was enthused about this book and this small town in Indiana, partly because of the interest in architecture in *his* family. When Sarah Jacobi changed positions at IU Press, editor Ashley Runyon took over this book, followed by project manager Nancy Lightfoot and Julia Turner of Amnet, who all worked to keep the author on track.

My thanks to my husband, David, who gave this manuscript a wise first reading and helped an English major (sort of) understand diesel engines. Thanks also to Marsh and Alyssa, the architects in the family, who actually understood what I was writing about, to Kate who kept the family fed, and to Madelyn who kept the computer (and operator) happily functioning.

A sad final note: as this manuscript was being finished, the iconic Time Inc. sign in lower Manhattan was taken down, to be put in storage likely forever. An overdue thanks, then, to the formidable Content Peckham, the patient and wise Liz Fremd, Marcia Gauger, and others in the Business Section at *Time*. They taught an eager young Midwesterner her craft in those days when women were researchers and only men could be writers. But who cared? The Time and Life Building was then on Forty-Ninth Street between Fifth and Sixth Avenues in Rockefeller Center across from the skating rink. It was the center of the journalistic universe.

PHOTO GALLERY

Each chapter opens with a photo of one of Columbus's iconic pieces of architecture or public art.

FAMILY TREE

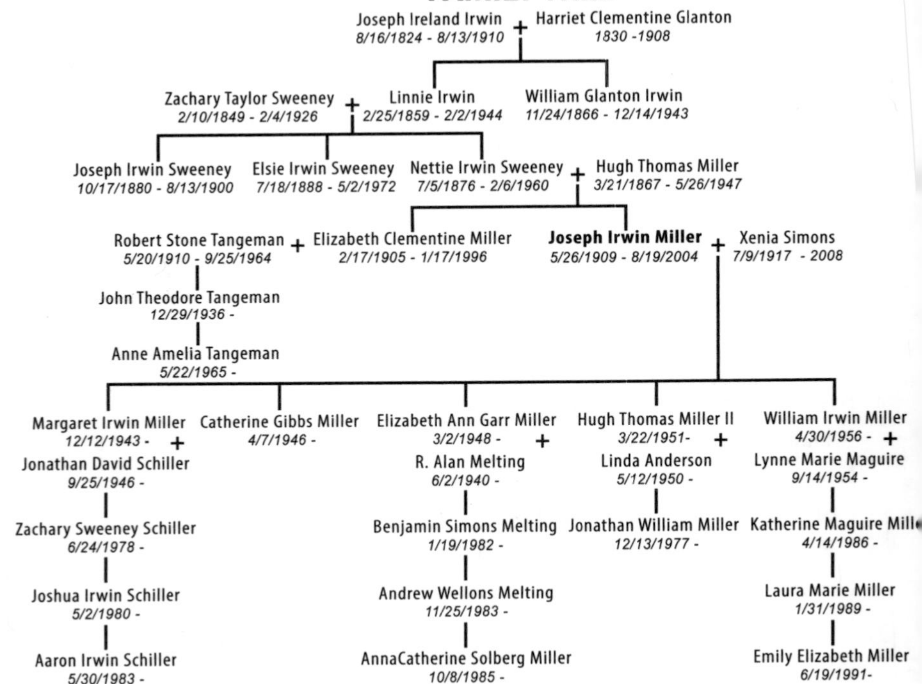

Joseph Ireland Irwin
8/16/1824 - 8/13/1910
+
Harriet Clementine Glanton
1830 -1908
Zachary Taylor Sweeney
2/10/1849 - 2/4/1926
+
Linnie Irwin
2/25/1859 - 2/2/1944
William Glanton Irwin
11/24/1866 - 12/14/1943
Joseph Irwin Sweeney
10/17/1880 - 8/13/1900
Elsie Irwin Sweeney
7/18/1888 - 5/2/1972
Nettie Irwin Sweeney
7/5/1876 - 2/6/1960
+
Hugh Thomas Miller
3/21/1867 - 5/26/1947
Robert Stone Tangeman
5/20/1910 - 9/25/1964
+
Elizabeth Clementine Miller
2/17/1905 - 1/17/1996
Joseph Irwin Miller
5/26/1909 - 8/19/2004
+
Xenia Simons
7/9/1917 - 2008
John Theodore Tangeman
12/29/1936 -
Anne Amelia Tangeman
5/22/1965 -
Margaret Irwin Miller
12/12/1943 -
+
Jonathan David Schiller
9/25/1946 -
Zachary Sweeney Schiller
6/24/1978 -
Joshua Irwin Schiller
5/2/1980 -
Aaron Irwin Schiller
5/30/1983 -
Catherine Gibbs Miller
4/7/1946 -
Elizabeth Ann Garr Miller
3/2/1948 -
+
R. Alan Melting
6/2/1940 -
Benjamin Simons Melting
1/19/1982 -
Andrew Wellons Melting
11/25/1983 -
AnnaCatherine Solberg Miller
10/8/1985 -
Hugh Thomas Miller II
3/22/1951-
+
Linda Anderson
5/12/1950 -
Jonathan William Miller
12/13/1977 -
William Irwin Miller
4/30/1956 -
+
Lynne Marie Maguire
9/14/1954 -
Katherine Maguire Mill
4/14/1986 -
Laura Marie Miller
1/31/1989 -
Emily Elizabeth Miller
6/19/1991-

J. IRWIN MILLER

First Christian Church, formerly Tabernacle Christian Church. Eliel Saarinen. 1942. *Balthazar Korab Archive, Library of Congress*

1 Lady Bird

THE PLANE WAS LATE. AT BAKALAR AIR FORCE BASE, WHERE THE welcoming party of dignitaries waited, Indiana's governor climbed back into his limousine, tipped his hat over his eyes, and took a quick nap. In the nearby town of Columbus, the people lining the streets waited more or less patiently as the gorgeous fall afternoon stretched into the light chill of evening. After all, how often did people living in rural America get a chance to be this close to the wife of the president of the United States?[1]

The point of Lady Bird Johnson's four-day, seven-state tour through the country's heartland in September 1967 was a bit more complicated than one of her normal beautification tours. Those trips showcased wildflowers and billboard-free interstates. This trip, this "Crossroads, USA" tour, was organized to demonstrate that small towns west of the Appalachians could be rewarding places to live.[2] The Johnson administration was said to be concerned that millions of Americans continued to pour into big cities, without properly appreciating life in some exemplary small towns.[3] Some also said that Lyndon B. Johnson (LBJ), under pressure from Vietnam War controversies, was trying to shore up his political support in the Midwest.

No place better illustrated the potential of small towns than Columbus, Indiana, the town that Lady Bird and her party were about to tour. Sleek, innovative modern buildings, many of them designed by some of the country's leading architects, had sprouted in this little town set among pastures and soybean fields in rural southern Indiana. This was no accident. It was the calculated strategy of the town's leading citizen—industrialist, scholar, arts patron, civil rights activist, and international religious lay leader Joseph Irwin Miller.

At last the buses, loaded with special guests, among them the architects who had designed these new buildings, pulled into Columbus, more than an hour behind schedule, and the people lining the sidewalks had their reward. An elderly woman bundled up against the evening air sat in a rocking chair on the sidewalk, waving. Another spectator had a sign reading "Welcome, Mrs. Johnson" tacked to one of her crutches.[4]

The buses drove slowly through the streets as tour guides pointed out structures of interest. At the suggestion of Liz Carpenter, Mrs. Johnson's energetic press secretary, a round of applause from the passengers went up for any architects present as the buses passed their buildings: Gunnar Birkerts and John Carl Warnecke for their elementary schools; Dan Kiley for commercial and residential landscapes and settings; Robert Venturi for Fire Station Number 4, under construction; and I. M. Pei and his associate Kenneth Carruthers for the partially completed county library. The works of architects who could not be present were also recognized: Edward Larrabee Barnes's Richards Elementary School and Harry Weese's church, schools, ice skating rink, and park. (Weese did not come into town on the buses but would join the group later.)

Notable among those missing were the two modern architectural giants who had started Columbus's architectural renaissance: Eliel Saarinen (1873–1950), whose elegantly spare Tabernacle Church of Christ with freestanding campanile (later the First Church of Christ) had been dedicated back in 1942, and his son, Eero Saarinen (1910–1961), who had helped his father with his work on the church and gone on to design a bank headquarters, another church, and two homes for the Irwin Miller family (one a summer home in Canada) before his early and sudden death following brain surgery.[5] Though the Saarinens designed only four buildings in Columbus, they established the aesthetics and tone for the innovative architectural spree that made it unlike any other small town in the United States.[6]

Modernism, that architectural style that flattened roofs and knocked gingerbread trim from buildings, made its way from Bauhaus to the United States in the early twentieth century with European immigrants such as Walter Gropius and Ludwig Mies van der Rohe. Eliel Saarinen, from Finland, was another talented practitioner and an exponent of the rational Finnish style, an example of which was his 1914 Helsinki Central Railway Station.[7] Many Americans learned about this puzzling but intriguing new way of building from the 1932 exhibit *Modern Architecture: International Exhibition* at the Museum of Modern Art in New York and the subsequent book *The International Style: Architecture Since 1922*. Organized by architect Philip Johnson, Henry-Russell Hitchcock, and several others, the show emphasized three tenets of modernism:

- Emphasis of volume over mass (planes rather than solidity)
- Rejection of symmetry
- Rejection of applied decoration[8]

These basic ideas, to one degree or another, would shape the buildings Lady Bird Johnson and her group would applaud as they rode in their buses through the streets of Columbus.

Some have likened the shape of the town of Columbus to an ice cream cone—narrow at the bottom, where the old part of town is squeezed between two rivers, and wide at the top, as new subdivisions, instead of soybeans, have sprouted on farmland north of town. But plenty of land is still farmed in the area around Columbus. The geography has not changed. There is a gentle roll to some of the land, though much of the terrain is tabletop flat, scraped smooth by glaciers a half million years ago. At least three times, glacial ice extended down into the land that would become Indiana. Those glaciers stopped just south of Columbus; to the south and west, hills, ridges, and ravines covered with giant stands of oak, hickory, and maple have made Brown County, Indiana, famously scenic.

Back in Bartholomew County, even the wide, fenceless farm fields north of Columbus have an openness that is nevertheless human scale. Clusters of yellow poplar and black walnut surround solitary farmhouses with their squat, round metal corn bins, though here and there a tall, stately, old-style silo is still in use. Trees stretch along the far horizons, a fringe of green in summer and a fringe of brown in winter, when leafless branches reach up and scratch a pewter sky. Unlike the lonesome, big-sky horizons of the West or the dusty bareness of the Southwest, this flat and open farmland is almost cozy.

These farms have abundant water for irrigation, since glaciers left the area with a high water table. These days the feathery arms of irrigation machinery stretch out over the fields like giant pterodactyls waiting to rise into the air, particularly in fields planted with seed corn and tomatoes for commercial canning. This abundance of water was part of what brought J. Irwin Miller's ancestors from Kentucky to settle and carve out farms in this part of the Midwest.

But Irwin Miller's great-grandfather Joseph Irwin decided there was more money to be made in selling supplies to farmers and their wives. As his Columbus dry goods store became a success, Irwin branched out into banking (his store had one of the only safes in town), real estate, roads and turnpikes, a tin plate company, a starch-refining company, and an interurban line. His son, William G. Irwin, continued to increase the family fortune, eventually putting money into a company to make the early diesel engines developed by Clessie Cummins, a local boy with a wide strain of ambition and mechanical genius.

❧ ❧ ❧

Even if Eliel and Eero Saarinen were both gone, the family did have a glamorous representative on hand for Lady Bird's Columbus event. Aline Saarinen, Eero's second wife and widow, was herself a respected art historian and architectural critic. Expanding her role as art critic for television's *Today* show, she had become the third woman reporter (after Pauline Frederick and Nancy Dickerson) for NBC News. Two months earlier, she had gone to St. Louis to attend a preopening inspection tour of the passenger system of the Gateway Arch designed by her late husband.[9]

At Eero Saarinen's hexagonal North Christian Church, with its dramatic, 192-foot needle spire piercing the sky and grounds designed by landscape architect Dan Kiley, everyone piled out of the buses for a quick tour and the official photograph. (Because of its roof, local wags called it "the oil can church.") As photographers got into position, the honored guests, chatting and looking about, stretched out in a line so endearingly sloppy that it would not have passed muster on the drawing tables of any of the design firms represented. John Dinkeloo and John Carl Warnecke bent down slightly to talk to Aline Saarinen, standing between them. Lady Bird Johnson and Muriel Humphrey, the country's First and Second Ladies, stood in the front row, smiling like good political wives. And just behind Lady Bird's shoulder, staring straight ahead, was square-jawed J. Irwin Miller, Cummins Engine Company chairman and host for this event.

It was Irwin Miller who had come up with the audacious plan to use architecture to upgrade the local school system, which, in turn, would make it easier to attract talent to Cummins. The importance of good architecture was detailed lyrically in a 1961 letter sent by Miller to the president of the Columbus school board. In it the Cummins Foundation renewed its earlier 1957 proposal to pay the school design fees of "first-rank" American architects. "Every one of us lives and moves all this life within the limitations, sight, and influence of architecture," wrote Miller. "The influence of architecture with which we are surrounded in our youth affects our lives, our standards, our tastes when we are grown, just as the influence of the parents and teachers with which we are surrounded affects us as adults." He continued, "American architecture has never had more creative, imaginative practitioners than it has today. Each of the best of today's architects can contribute something of lasting value to Columbus."[10] It is interesting to note that some critics (for instance, *Architectural Forum*'s Peter Blake) were beginning to feel that in becoming an architectural style, modernism had lost its original Bauhaus reform soul. And yet here in America's heartland, Irwin Miller had put modernism to the service of school reform.

The school project was about more than just architecture. It also had to do with the importance of quality over mediocrity, of how all people in Columbus, not just the leading citizens, should have access to good design. It pulled together many of the things Miller thought were important. Deep down Miller could even have had a religious motivation—to protect the dignity of all God's children. The school program had in turn influenced the design of other buildings in Columbus. After all, no one wanted to look like an out-of-date bumpkin when the building across the street or around the corner was a sexy harbinger of the future. By 1967 there were fifteen innovative modern structures for Lady Bird and the other dignitaries to admire as their buses rolled around town.

Then it was time for dinner. Appropriately, John Carl Warnecke's peak-roofed McDowell Elementary School was the setting for "A Salute to Columbus Architecture," to which one hundred local Columbus couples had also been invited. The five-year-old McDowell Elementary, built in 1962, was the second school for which the architectural fees had been funded by the Cummins Foundation. It would later be named a National Historic Landmark.

Warnecke, based in San Francisco, had studied under Walter Gropius at Harvard. He was known for "contextualism"—respecting existing surroundings when designing a new building. In Indiana he had been influenced visually by the rural terrain: flat farm fields punctuated by tall structures—lean, two-story, white-frame farmhouses, silos, barns, and clumps of trees. His McDowell School used a "cluster plan," in which groups of classrooms around a central, taller common building were linked through trellised walkways to an interior courtyard and other open areas. The classrooms were placed in small clusters because Warnecke wanted the school to have a safe, welcoming atmosphere for small children who were perhaps venturing from their snug homes into the outside world for the first time.

Some of the architects had been selected for their Columbus commissions early in their careers, or at least before their most famous works were done. The McDowell School project was commissioned years before Warnecke worked with Jackie Kennedy to integrate government buildings into the historic facade of Washington's Lafayette Square or before he later designed JFK's grave site in Arlington National Cemetery. Harry Weese, a prolific Chicago architect who had studied at Cranbrook with Eliel Saarinen, had designed the first of the modern Columbus schools in 1957. Years later, he began work on the Washington, DC, Metro system, finally completed in 1976—a network of stations deemed by critic Herbert Muschamp to be among the greatest public works of the twentieth century. I. M. Pei's brick county library in Columbus was still under construction during the 1967 Lady Bird visit. Twenty years later, his glass pyramid addition to the Louvre would astonish Parisians and tourists.

Wearing a ruby-red velvet evening coat, Lady Bird charmed many with the toast she made during the gala evening.[11] "It is said that architecture is frozen music, but seldom in history has any group of devoted artists produced such a symphony in stone as presents itself to the eye in Columbus," she said. "I am deeply touched by what I have seen. Thank you for giving your genius and your heart to make this part of America more beautiful."[12]

After dining outside at round tables set up in the McDowell School's courtyard, the guests moved to the adjacent, magically transformed basketball court. There they were entertained with portions of the American National Opera Company's production of Verdi's *Falstaff*, with a sixty-piece orchestra and the formidable Sarah Caldwell conducting.

And then to bed. It was after midnight before the First Lady and her hosts, Irwin and Xenia Miller, retired to the low, glass-and-marble Miller home designed by Eero Saarinen, Kevin Roche, and Alexander Girard, a house that fifty years later would be considered one of the most important masterworks of twentieth-century modernism. Lady Bird would later record in her diary, "One of my personal self-indulgences while in this house [the White House] has been to arrange a quiet visit with . . . businessmen who have made a special mark on our country's life, such as Tom Watson [the president of IBM] or Irwin Miller."[13] Elsewhere in town, Aline Saarinen, the overnight guest of Cummins president Don Tull and his wife, was still up working on coverage of the events for NBC television's flagship evening news show, the *Huntley-Brinkley Report*.

At 6:30 the following morning, the phone rang at Irwin and Xenia Miller's house. It was President Johnson calling. He asked that his wife call him when she woke up. You are getting good press, he told her when she returned his call. Having the country's First Lady as a houseguest added a few new elements to the Miller family's morning routine.[14] Secret Service agents spent the night at the end of the Miller driveway, surprising a young neighbor, Matt Callaway, when he pedaled up for his regular bike ride to school with his eleven-year-old friend, Will Miller. After Matt had been cleared, Will took him out to the patio to meet Mrs. Johnson, who was having breakfast with his parents and who graciously chatted with the two boys. Later that day, Matt would go home early from school—possibly suffering from the stress of encounters not only with the Secret Service but also with the First Lady of the land.[15]

It might have been Lady Bird Johnson's first visit to Columbus, but her husband, Lyndon Johnson, and Irwin Miller were well acquainted. The president had appointed Miller to presidential committees and commissions concerning money and credit, trade with eastern Europe and the Soviet Union, urban housing, postal organization, and the US policy toward southern Africa. More important, Miller had been Johnson's staunch ally in promoting civil rights legislation as first lay president of the sometimes-controversial National Council of Churches.

The following month's *Esquire* magazine carried a long, flattering article on J. Irwin Miller, including his picture in solemn profile on the cover along with the line, "This man ought to be the next President of the United States."[16] As part of his preliminary research, the *Esquire* article's author, Steven V. Roberts, a Washington political reporter, began talking to people about "this fellow Miller" out in Indiana and his qualifications as a Republican presidential candidate.

In disbelief, Roberts wrote, "I began thinking that this could not be J. Irwin Miller. It was Spencer Tracy playing J. Irwin Miller—a figment craftily contrived by a team of highly paid scriptwriters to meet my precise requirements." Miller, wrote Roberts, "reads the New Testament in Greek (he also reads Latin) and for years was a substitute Sunday School teacher. For relaxation [he] plays Bach on his Stradivarius, drives a speedboat and plays golf on a new public course he recently donated to the city."

"Wouldn't Irwin Miller be great?" New York City mayor John Lindsay had said to Roberts when they were discussing possible GOP presidential candidates. "He's one of the great people of this world. He's got insight, humor, wisdom, saltiness."[17] Of course, it was not to be. An Irwin Miller boomlet never developed. Miller, a lifelong Republican, threw his support to Nelson Rockefeller, who lost to Richard Nixon in the Republican primary. Nixon eventually defeated Democratic candidate Hubert Humphrey for the presidency.

"Never forget where you came from," Miller told Roberts during their interview for the *Esquire* article. "This doesn't make you a conservative, this doesn't make you always want to go back to something, but this gives you your base." And then Miller quoted what he called an "electric" phrase from the Roman historian Tacitus: "praiseworthy competition with one's ancestors." To Miller this meant "making an objective, realistic appraisal of the accomplishments of ancestors, understanding how difficult an achievement these were . . . and a determination to see if you can't do something comparable under your own circumstances."

"Irwin Miller is a private man," observed Roberts. "He is usually out of town one night a week but tries to spend most weekends in Columbus. . . . When it [the clock in his office] reaches five-thirty, Miller usually gets up to leave for home. 'When I'm in town we always have dinner together. . . . Everything revolves around that.'" Roberts continued, "Miller is essentially a pragmatist. . . . You do what works, not what is supposed to work under some preconceived notion. Ways of solving problems must change as conditions change, if you are going to pursue effectively the same basic ends."

The *Esquire* article, combined with the national coverage of Lady Bird's visit, caused people around the country who track such things to ask, Just who is this man Miller anyway? For an answer to that and an understanding of what influences produced this broadly accomplished man—in some sense a modern Medici—it is necessary to go back to 1846 and the arrival in Columbus of the first of his family, Joseph I. Irwin.

7
46

Robert N. Stewart Bridge entry into Columbus. J. Muller International. 1999. *Carol M. Highsmith, Library of Congress*

2 Joseph

IN THE SUMMER OF 1846, EARLY RISERS ALONG THE DUSTY ROADS running south from the village of Edinburgh, Indiana, could often catch a glimpse of an energetic young man hiking the four miles into the nearby Bartholomew County seat of Columbus. He could have ridden, of course. The Madison and Indianapolis Railroad connected the two towns, and his mother had given him the fare of thirty cents.[1] But if he walked to his new job at Snyder & Alden's dry goods store in Columbus, he could save that thirty cents. Sometimes he walked part of the way barefoot, his shoes slung over his shoulder. For saving—whether money or shoe leather—was what it was all about for twenty-two-year-old Joseph Ireland Irwin, who was set on making his mark in the world.

Joe Irwin was not the first farm boy to decide to head for the city, leaving behind the grindingly hard work of clearing land and battling weather, weeds, and insects. Like Dick Wittington, he arrived in town with nothing and by the end of his life was the most powerful and respected man in town. He came to believe that for the new country to prosper, its people should manufacture more goods, import less, and live within their means.[2]

The Irwins had been among the pioneer families settling the new state of Indiana that had been carved out of the Old Northwest Territory in 1816. Joe Irwin's grandfather, also a Joseph, had been an immigrant from Ireland, the mostly Protestant north, and had fought in the Indian wars under General "Mad" Anthony Wayne. In 1828 the family had moved from Kentucky up into Indiana along with many others, often small farmers who were morally opposed to slavery or unwilling or unable to compete against the free slave labor on larger Kentucky farms.

Like many in nineteenth-century America, the young and ambitious Joe Irwin used land as a way to latch onto the bottom rungs of the ladder of success. Three years after starting work in Columbus, a village with a population under one thousand at the junction of the East Branch of the White River and Haw Creek, Joe Irwin and a partner bought 135 acres of farmland adjoining the town. It was the first of many real estate purchases. Many years later, Joseph Irwin was said to own nearly all of Columbus north of Fifth Street.

By 1850 Joseph Irwin had saved enough money to open his own store. His letterhead advertised "Wholesale and Retail Dealer in Dry Goods, Boots, Shoes, Carpet, Hats, Notions, &c, &c."[3] Because his store at the corner of Washington and Fourth Streets had one of the only safes in town, customers began bringing their extra cash to him for safekeeping. This evolved into full-time banking, and in 1871 Irwin's Bank was chartered, with Joseph Irwin as president. In later years he would say that if an industrious young man would begin at the age of twenty-one to save and invest one-fourth of his earnings, he would be a rich man at fifty. He had followed his own advice. The seeds of land, banking, and commerce that Joseph Irwin planted in the last half of the nineteenth century grew the Irwin-Sweeney-Miller family fortune.

In 1850, the same year he opened his dry goods store, Joseph Irwin married Harriet Clementine Glanton, a young girl from the Columbus area. Religion—an important factor in the life of one of

Joseph Irwin's twentieth-century descendants, J. Irwin Miller—was a prominent aspect of the family's life from the beginning. In 1823 family members helped start New Hope, a little log church in the Bartholomew County countryside. It was first affiliated with the Baptist denomination, but later became an independent Christian church. (The denomination would later be known as the Disciples of Christ.) In 1855 sixty members split off from the New Hope Church to organize the Christian Congregation in Columbus.[4] Joseph Irwin served as secretary-treasurer.

The rumblings of the war between the North and South reverberated in Columbus and through all of southern Indiana, where many people had Southern roots. A camp rendezvous, where troops and supplies could be assembled, was established on the outskirts of Columbus. Many answered the governor's call for volunteers to protect the state against Southern invaders. "Farmers left their grain to rot in the fields, mechanics dropped their tools, merchants abandoned their stores, professional men their desks, clerks forgot their ledgers and students their textbooks, and young and old alike all swarmed in constantly thickening throngs to the capital or the nearest place of rendezvous," described a dramatic report of the state's adjutant general.[5]

The folks at home worried about the progress of Morgan's Raiders, the Confederate cavalry unit under the command of Brig. Gen. John Hunt Morgan rampaging through Kentucky, southern Indiana, and Ohio during the summer of 1863. Corydon, Salem, Vernon, Versailles—would Columbus be in his path?

In the town of Dupont, Indiana, two counties over from Columbus, Morgan's men burned the town's storehouse and "liberated" two thousand smoked hams, which were later discarded along the side of the road when they began attracting flies. As it turned out, Morgan's men came within twenty miles of Columbus before heading east to Ohio where, in late July 1863, they were captured by Federal troops.[6]

Joseph Irwin, at thirty-seven, was too old to serve as a soldier. Governor Oliver Morton, however, called on Irwin, a prosperous citizen of southern Indiana, for advice from time to time. At war's end, Irwin, representing the Third Congressional District, was appointed to the board of directors of the new Home for Disabled Soldiers located in Knightstown.[7]

War or no war, Joseph Irwin built a larger home on tree-lined Fifth Street in 1864. His family had grown; they had welcomed a baby girl, Linnie, in 1859. The additional room proved welcome when a baby boy, William Glanton Irwin, arrived in 1866. The house, with its low-pitched roof and wrought-iron trim (including a railing around a small widow's walk on the roof), was Italianate in design and made of brick, like several other new houses in the neighborhood and many Columbus buildings. In 1884 a veranda was added on the east side of the house.[8] The original structure would be enlarged and renovated again in 1910 and an extensive garden would be added. Other additions would expand the house through the years to accommodate more generations of the Irwin-Sweeney-Miller family.

William G. (W. G.) Irwin, Joseph and Harriet's son, would live most of his life in this constantly expanding house. Later circumstances would make W. G. Irwin the predominant father figure in the life of his great-nephew, J. Irwin Miller. W. G. Irwin attended Columbus public schools and then Butler College in Indianapolis. He was persuaded to move back home into the large brick house on Fifth Street, where he could have his own bachelor quarters in the third-floor tower. During the summer and vacations from school, he worked for his father at the bank, and after graduation he became cashier and joined his father in several business enterprises.[9]

In 1871, a lanky young minister arrived in town to become pastor of the Disciples Church, which was located down the street from the Irwin house. Zachary Taylor (Z. T.) Sweeney was born in Kentucky to a father who was a minister and a mother whose maiden name was Campbell. She was said to be related to Alexander Campbell, the famous preacher who had helped several denominations of the Reformed tradition (principally Presbyterians and Disciples of Christ) gain a foothold in the developing middle part of the country.

Z. T. Sweeney was friendly and personable, had a strong voice and imposing presence in the pulpit, and preached sermons that were easy to follow. He often used stories to illustrate thorny spiritual dilemmas. Theologically conservative, he was nevertheless ready to listen to other points of view. Many years later, he would be the person to whom his grandson, J. Irwin Miller, would turn with theological questions.[10] The congregation thrived and grew, and in 1879 dedicated a new building and took a new name: Tabernacle Church of Christ.

It was inevitable that the young minister would become well acquainted with the Irwin family, a strong presence in the congregation. After several years in Columbus, Sweeney was called to church pulpits further south, though Columbus was obviously not forgotten. In 1875, the twenty-six-year-old pastor returned from Atlanta, Georgia, to marry the Irwins' sixteen-year-old daughter, Linnie. A daughter, Nettie Sweeney, was born a year later in 1876, followed by a son, Joseph, in 1880, and another daughter, Elsie, in 1888. All three children were given the middle name "Irwin."

Z. T. and Linnie Sweeney's marriage may have had its occasional rough spots, with Linnie Sweeney appearing to be closer to her extended Irwin family than to her husband, whom she addressed as "Mr. Sweeney." She once told her grandson, perhaps facetiously, that the reason she married so young was so she could go to a popular ice cream parlor on the town square anytime she wanted without having to ask her mother.[11]

Nineteenth-century Bartholomew County Courthouse reflected in twentieth-century Columbus glass. Isaac Hodgson. 1874.
Don Nissen, Columbus Visitors Center

3 Muskoka

FIRST CAME THE FISH—WALLEYE PIKE, SMALLMOUTH BASS, AND lake trout. Then came the First Peoples—primarily Ojibwa and Chippewa—who used the area as hunting grounds. Then the nineteenth-century fish camps—canvas tents in which city ladies in long skirts, shirtwaists, and, of course, hats, cast their own fishing lines or tended cooking fires in preparation for the fish their men, equally formally dressed in three-piece suits, would wrest from the cold lake waters. Eventually the tents were replaced by sturdier buildings, repurposed frame farmhouses and shingle-style Victorian cottages.

Many of these cottages are still standing in the twenty-first century, occupied each summer by descendants of those hardy vacationers who fled the summer heat in Toronto, New York, Cleveland, Pittsburgh, and the American Midwest and headed north by train and lake steamer to the thick forests and sparkling lakes curving along the east edge of Lake Huron's Georgian Bay in an area called Muskoka.

One of Z. T. Sweeney's great passions was fishing—tarpon in Florida and freshwater varieties in the cold waters of the north. (Many years later he would be appointed Indiana's commissioner of fisheries and game.) In 1876 Sweeney discovered Muskoka in Canada's Ontario province, a region spotted with three big lakes—Muskoka, Joseph, and Rosseau—and a sprinkling of little towns. This discovery would have an impact on several generations of Irwins, Sweeneys, and Millers, who came to love the heavy forests and cool waters to which they could escape each summer.

Sweeney soon convinced family members and friends to join him on his trips to Canada. It was said that the men and children enjoyed the rustic fishing-camp experience, but the women in the family, not so much.[1] A large photograph dated 1886 shows Sweeney, wide-brimmed hat pushed back, standing in the midst of a dozen-plus men, women, and children on a rough hillside in front of a tent or two. Lake Joseph is in the background. In his right hand Sweeney holds one end of a line on which the day's fish catch is proudly displayed for the camera.

His wife, Linnie, is off to the side, a wisp of a smile on her face. Their son, little tow-headed Joe Sweeney, sits on the ground in front of his father; Nettie Sweeney stands farther up the hill holding a long oar, the brim of her sun hat turned back. W. G. Irwin, Linnie Sweeney's brother, stands behind Z. T. Sweeney on the left, looking off into the distance, his thumb hooked into a belt loop. At twenty, the dark-haired, sturdy, and good-looking W. G. (also known as Will) Irwin would continue his studies at Butler College in the fall.

In 1906 Z. T. Sweeney found a cottage to rent in the area. The women in the family presumably had agreed that the beauty of the area made it worth putting up with some backwoods inconveniences. Three years later, in 1909, Sweeney's father-in-law, Joseph I. Irwin, purchased an estate on Lake Rosseau, just outside the handful of shops, cottages, and summer hotels that made up the small town of Windermere. The extended Irwin-Sweeney family would vacation here for many future decades.

Llanllar, the name of Joseph Irwin's property, came from a Welsh village important to the family of the original owner, and the Miller family would continue the tradition by naming later cottages they built on the property after Welsh villages. One entrance to the property abutted the fashionable summer hotel Windermere, a classic type of lodging that Canadians and East Coast Americans had been visiting in the summer for decades, with Adirondack chairs (here called Muskoka chairs) lined up across the front lawn to catch breezes from the lake. Getting to the property in the days before roads and automobiles was part of the adventure. In later years Irwin Miller would remember a "little, old wood-burning train that had kerosene lamps hanging from the roof of the day-coach" and the evocative smells of the last section of the journey by boat: "the hot paint on the boiler and of the steam engine, then of the water, then of the pines along the lakeshore."[2]

By that point, owning a summer estate in Canada was no stretch for the Irwin family. Joseph Irwin, the paterfamilias, had shown a sure touch in seizing on business opportunities in the developing state of Indiana—even if parts of northern and central Indiana were developing more rapidly than Columbus and the rest of southern Indiana.[3] Having sold his retail dry goods business in 1891, Joseph Irwin had become a full-time banker, with the available capital to invest. W. G. Irwin, who had worked summers at the Irwin bank, joined his father in business activities after graduating from Butler in 1889.

Local investment opportunities arose from protective tariffs, an important factor in the national election of 1888. One of these tariffs meant a new duty on imported tin, beginning in 1890. Tin covered the iron sheets from which "tin" cans were made to hold the fruit and vegetables available on American tables beyond the growing season. Previously, the United States had imported tin, mainly from Wales. Joseph and W. G. organized the Union Tinplate Company with factories in Anderson, Indiana, in the heart of the state's natural gas region, and in Pennsylvania. After a few years, these factories were sold, and W. G. Irwin encouraged his father to invest in the growing interurban industry, key to improving transportation in the country's midsection.[4]

By 1895 Columbus was one of eleven Indiana towns with electric-powered, trolley-like cars running down the middle of its streets. Power was delivered by an electric third rail running down the middle of the track. More importantly, the electric-powered cars began providing transportation between towns. Another visible sign of the town's growing importance was the handsome Bartholomew County Courthouse, finished in 1874. Designed by Indianapolis architect Isaac Hodgson, the Second Empire–style building would become known as one of the state's most beautiful courthouses.[5]

For some years Joseph Irwin, originally a Whig, had been involved in the activities of the new Republican Party, serving as a delegate to the party's national conventions in 1872 and 1884 and working within the party for the presidential nomination and eventual election of Benjamin Harrison in 1888. Harrison, born in Ohio, served at the time as US senator from Indiana. He would become the country's twenty-third president. That support paid off and may well have added a cosmopolitan touch to household dinner table conversations in later years. The lives, personalities, and activities of family members would be particularly important in the future development of young Irwin Miller, since four generations of Irwins, Sweeneys, and Millers would eventually live together in the big brick house on Fifth Street.

In August 1889 President Harrison named Z. T. Sweeney (more formally, the Reverend Zachary Sweeney) American consul general in Constantinople, capital of the Ottoman Empire. (Ankara would not become Turkey's capital until 1923, and the Turkish government did not insist on using the name Istanbul until the 1930s.) However, the real push for Z. T. Sweeney's appointment had come from elsewhere. Three years earlier, in 1886, a powerful and respected member of the Disciples church, Isaac Errett, editor of the denomination's newspaper, *Christian Standard,* had been given a "purse" for a trip abroad by grateful supporters to visit the areas in the Middle East that he had written about and dreamed of visiting for so many years. Casting about for a "genial and intelligent traveling companion," he chose Zachary Sweeney, pastor of the Disciples church in Columbus, Indiana.[6]

After returning from the extensive trip, Sweeney wrote the book *Under Ten Flags* about the experience. The travelers had visited Constantinople, where the Disciples of Christ supported a missionary for several years. The Turkish government had made it nearly impossible to proselytize Muslims, so Christian missionaries, including the Disciples, did their work among Armenians and Orthodox Christians.[7]

Sweeney sprinkled his book with classical references—Jason and the Argonauts and Odysseus and his trials and temptations. Sometimes these lent themselves to personal moral asides. When Odysseus came to the island of the Sirens, wrote Rev. Sweeney, he "prevented himself from being led astray by putting wax in his ears and binding himself to the mast." Added Sweeney, who had been away from Linnie and his little family in Columbus for half a year: "Happy is the Christian on life's troubled sea, that has sweeter music at home than can be found in the siren song of temptation."[8] Some letters home were on letterheads of the Consulate General of the United States of America/Constantinople. "My darling wife," Sweeney had written in the spring of 1887, "never for a moment has my affection been diminished or cooled for you. . . . We have had our little differences but like thunder showers they have cleaned the atmosphere of life and made it the brighter. As ever and forever, your loving husband."[9]

Sweeney apparently wore well as a traveling companion on the six-month trip, for Errett later wrote President Harrison recommending Sweeney as the official American consul general. The forty-year-old Sweeney's new appointment to the Constantinople post was greeted with great enthusiasm in many quarters. Said the popular publication *Frank Leslie's Illustrated Newspaper*, "President Harrison has made one appointment which gives universal satisfaction in his own State, to Jackson Democrats as well as Lincoln Republicans, that of Rev. Dr. Z. T. Sweeney, L.L.D., Chancellor of the Butler University and editor-in-chief of the *Central Christian*, to be Consul-General to the Turkish Empire." Dr. Sweeney, continued the effusive article, "is an eloquent and forcible speaker, as well as a chaste and trenchant writer, in the prime of vigorous manhood, physically active and mentally bright, a student not only of books, but of men as well, possessing a mind enlarged by travel and familiarity with peoples of different nationalities, good executive ability, and of excellent judgment and business tact."[10]

By Christmas 1889 most of Zachary Sweeney's family had joined him in Constantinople: Linnie, baby Elsie, and nine-year-old Joe, whose education Sweeney was overseeing at the consulate. Only the eldest, thirteen-year-old Nettie, remained in Columbus. After several years of attending diplomatic garden parties and representing American interests in Turkey, the Sweeney family returned to Indiana. Following family tradition, Nettie and younger brother, Joe, both headed for Butler College. Nettie graduated in 1898. There she met the man she would soon marry, Hugh Miller, a professor of history and French who had studied in Europe.

With marriage into the Columbus family on the horizon, Hugh Miller left academia and came to Columbus to join the Irwin bank as cashier and eventually as vice president. Nettie Sweeney, twenty-four, and Hugh Miller, thirty-three, were married at the end of 1900, though this would be the only bright spot in a year stained by a family tragedy.

❧ ❧ ❧

The White River at the west end of Third Street was a popular Columbus swimming hole, an area known as "high banks." Nineteen-year-old Joe Sweeney, soon to be a senior at Butler, was working at the Irwin bank for the summer. On a Monday night in mid-August 1900, he headed for a swim after work with two friends. A good swimmer, Joe leapt or dived from the eight-foot cliff into the water. He told his friends he was going to see how long he could hold his breath. When he came to the surface, he was floating face down, his friends later reported. Then his body, seized by the slow current, moved out into the deeper part of the river and disappeared. Some small boys playing on the bank were sent into town to sound the alarm. In the gathering dusk, a large group of men and boys searched the river, Joe's father Z. T. Sweeney among them. The body was finally found and pulled from the river. For several hours, by lantern light, several of the town's doctors tried without success to revive him.[11]

An outstanding student and campus leader, Joe was mourned by his high school and college classmates, but he was also mourned much more widely. Letters to the family mentioned the great promise shown by the heir apparent and predictions that he would have been an impressive citizen and contributor to his town, his state, and his country. The outpouring of sympathy included a note to the family from President Benjamin Harrison. Even a Greek newspaper carried an item about the tragedy, identifying him as the son of the former consul in Constantinople. Said an editorial in the Indianapolis Sun, "The child and grandchild of wealthy and cultured parents, there was scarcely another youth in the state who had such advantages backed by so much natural ability. It is impossible to measure such a loss."[12]

The funeral was held at the home of Joe's grandparents on Fifth Street where extra chairs and decorations were already in place. Ironically, preparations had been underway for a party to celebrate the fiftieth wedding anniversary of Joseph and Harriet Irwin.

Northside Middle School.
Harry Weese. 1961.
Carol M. Highsmith, Library of Congress

4 Irwin

IT STRUCK SOME OF THE FAMILY AS ODD. ON RETURNING FROM A cruise around the Canadian lake in his motor launch with other members of the family, the spry family patriarch, eighty-six-year-old Joseph Irwin, headed for the room in the family's Muskoka cottage where his fifteen-month-old great-grandson, Joseph Irwin Miller, was sleeping. His granddaughter, Nettie Sweeney Miller, followed, thinking that perhaps he did not know her baby was asleep. "I just want to see the boy one more time," he said. He stood and looked at his tiny namesake for a long time. The following day the old man became ill with what was thought to be pneumonia. Two days later he died. Perhaps he had had a premonition of his approaching death, family members thought later.[1]

The baby, Joseph Irwin Miller, had been born a year earlier, May 26, 1909, the second child of Nettie and Hugh Miller. His older sister, Elizabeth Clementine Miller, had been born four years earlier. Siblings Irwin and Clementine (pronounced *Cle-men-teen*) would be lifelong friends and dependable supporters of one another. Perhaps the family's position—which at times created a subtle isolation from other children in town, at least in Irwin's case—reinforced their bond.

The body of Joseph Irwin, Columbus's "most prominent citizen," was brought from Canada back to Columbus, and nearly a hundred Columbus businessmen gathered at the train station to meet the funeral party. (His wife, Harriet, had died two years earlier.) The casket was taken to the south parlor of the family home for viewing and then to the Tabernacle Christian Church for the funeral. A black-bordered sketch on the front page of the local newspaper showed a woman labeled "Columbus," head down in grief, leaning on a draped casket, in front of which were wreaths labeled "Sympathy, Honor, Fame and Love." At 3:00 p.m. cars on the Indianapolis, Columbus & Southern Traction line stopped where they were for five minutes in a show of respect for the company's founder.[2]

With four generations having lived together in the brick mansion on Fifth Street (as townspeople referred to it), a bright little boy like Irwin Miller could easily absorb the values and philosophies in which he was marinating. There was his great-grandfather, though Irwin was only a baby when he died, and his grandparents, Z. T. and Linnie Sweeney, when they were not in Istanbul or filling interim, out-of-town church pulpits. There was his great-uncle, W. G. Irwin, whose bachelor quarters were in the tower at the front of the house looking down on Fifth Street; his parents, Nettie and Hugh Miller; his aunt, Nettie's maiden sister, Elsie Sweeney; and his older sister, Clementine.

Hugh Thomas Miller, the father of Clementine and Irwin, was born on a farm in a county northwest of Columbus and was also the son of a minister. The two Disciples of Christ ministers (John Chapman Miller and Z. T. Sweeney) knew and respected each other. Both were remarkably well educated for the rural Midwest in the mid-1800s. John Miller, having studied law briefly before deciding on the ministry, taught at Northwestern Christian University before it was renamed Butler. The senior Miller could read several languages and educated Hugh and his brothers and sisters at home, in addition to farming and preaching at churches in the area. Irwin Miller's forbearers were not lazy layabouts.[3]

Like his father, Hugh Miller had a scholarly bent. After graduating from Butler he taught there—languages and history. However, interspersed with his years on the faculty, he had gone to Europe to study at the Sorbonne in Paris (where he wrote a thesis on Victor Hugo) and in Vienna. He landed in Vienna during its musical golden age and had the opportunity to see and hear Brahms and Strauss perform, he later proudly told his family. His interest in serious music would flow down to future generations. While in Europe, Hugh Miller, in his mid-twenties, grew a red, pointed Van Dyke beard and lived an almost operatic life of the impecunious student. At one point he lived in an unheated flat where he had to soak his feet in pans of hot water to get warm. A resulting case of pleurisy weakened his lungs, and, thought family members, possibly contributed to serious health problems later in his life.[4]

Throughout his life Hugh Miller loved learning. Irwin Miller remembered his father jumping up from the dinner table to find an encyclopedia if a question came up about which he wanted an answer—immediately. Irwin Miller grew up assuming his father knew everything. When he was about ten years old, Irwin Miller was shocked the first time he heard his father say, "I don't know," in answer to a question. Hugh Miller's knowledge and scholarship were so well-known that even the local newspaper editor called occasionally to double-check facts in the midst of writing an editorial.

Nettie Miller had long since lost her schoolgirl awe of her scholarly husband by the time her son Irwin came along. Irwin Miller once overheard his mother talking to a female friend. "Mr. Miller is surely the smartest man I know," said the friend. "Yes, and he is not entirely unaware of the fact," replied his wife.[5]

Politics was another of Hugh Miller's interests. Despite his position at the bank and involvement in other family enterprises (among them Union Starch and Refining and the interurban line), he had time to serve in the Indiana General Assembly and as Indiana's lieutenant governor from 1905 to 1909. The family, particularly his father-in-law, Z. T., encouraged this movement into politics.[6] Hugh Miller made an unsuccessful run for the US Senate in 1914. Two years later he launched a second campaign for the Senate, but a health crisis interfered, dashing all ambitions for future state or national office. He was diagnosed with tuberculosis (TB). The family speculated that pleurisy during his student days in Europe may have made him vulnerable to this infectious disease that, at the time, was the second-leading cause of death in Indiana, behind heart disease.[7]

Battle Creek Sanitarium in Michigan and the Trudeau Sanitarium at Saranac Lake in New York's Adirondack Mountains were among America's foremost TB sanitariums. Hugh Miller went to both places for treatment, which, in pre-streptomycin days, consisted primarily of rest, wholesome food, rest, fresh air, sunshine, and rest.[8] With Hugh gone from Columbus much of the time, Irwin Miller's great-uncle W. G. Irwin in some ways became a father figure to his nephew Irwin, who was now the family heir after Joe Sweeney's tragic drowning.

When Irwin Miller was growing up, other boys from the neighborhood would sometimes congregate in the family's backyard, which held the neighborhood's only basketball goal. Yet in the 1980s, when Irwin Miller recorded memories of his boyhood, he remembered only two friends. (Clementine, he noted, "made friends more easily than I did.")[9] One of Irwin's friends, Ray Eddy, would go on to become a well-known name in basketball—*the* sport in Indiana, particularly small-town Indiana. Ray Eddy was a star basketball player at Columbus High School and Purdue University, a state championship–winning coach at Madison High School (Indiana), and later the men's basketball coach for fifteen years at Purdue. Irwin Miller spent much of his time at the nearby Eddy house, where Mrs. Eddy would fix the boys sorghum molasses on white bread—"and I still love the taste," wrote Irwin Miller decades later.[10] The boys spent much time trying to stay out of the way of Irwin's older sister and her giggling friends. They wore knickerbockers (knickers), pants that buckled just above the knee, paired with black cotton stockings, which were sometimes a bit the worse for an active boy's wear. "My grandmother (Sweeney) spent much of her time darning these and other stockings, especially around the knees."[11]

Grandmother Sweeney did much of her mending in an upstairs sewing room that looked down on the garden. The house's extensive Italian gardens, designed by Arthur Shurcliff and part of the 1910 remodeling, were open to the public. Teenagers sometimes stopped in the garden for a little hugging and kissing on the way home from school. Linnie Sweeney was always alert to these amorous shenanigans and would rap sharply on the window with her thimble if she spotted such goings on.[12]

Much of Irwin's early education had come at the family dinner table. With the family's strong tradition of ministers in the family, there was much discussion of religion. Dinner table topics also included such political questions as the importance of a strong protective tariff and women's suffrage (the men in the family seemed to support this more than the women).[13] Adults at the table were supportive of rights for black people, and most frowned upon anti-Semitic remarks, attitudes that influenced Clementine and Irwin Miller. Aunt Elsie, however, was an exception. Though she was at home in the world of classical music, she once commented sotto voce, "You know, Toscanini is really a Jew." Irwin Miller remembered thinking at the time, What has that got to do with anything? When the Royal Muskoka Hotel went bankrupt and Jewish investors reportedly sought to buy it, it was primarily Elsie Sweeney who pushed a chagrined W. G. Irwin into joining the rest of the cottage owners in buying hotel shares to prevent the sale, though he had close Jewish friends at home in Columbus.[14]

Irwin Miller's school grades were acceptable but not as good as his sister's, as he remembered it.[15] After eight years in Columbus public schools, Irwin Miller was sent East to boarding school at the age of fourteen. His sister, Clementine, was already in the East at Smith. The Taft School in Watertown, Connecticut, had been founded in 1890 by the brother of US president William Howard Taft. The boys (girls would not attend there until 1972) were expected to dress in coat and tie for dinner and to attend Vespers before dinner and church on Sunday. The school's motto was *Non ut sibi ministretur sed ut minister*—not to be served but to serve—appropriate for educating a young man much later described as a "man of honesty, high purpose and intelligence" in an *Esquire* article touting him as a candidate for president of the United States.[16] Irwin Miller may have left the lofty, religious dinner table conversations back in Columbus, Indiana, but he had not left a noblesse oblige attitude about life in general—to whom much has been given, from them is much expected.

At Taft, "J. I." Miller participated in activities ranging from debate to basketball, but music remained a dominant interest—four years in the concert orchestra and the following lines in the school annual his senior year: "Have you never heard of a Sabbath morn, down lecture-hall way, the aristocratic tones of a real Stradivarius?"[17] Irwin and roommate Maynard Mack wrote the words and music to a song, "Some Other Day," published in *The Oracle*, the school student literary magazine, during their senior year.[18]

It was a solid education for the young scholar, no matter how much he might have missed home. "Dear Unk," he wrote in a letter home to W. G. Irwin, "Thanks ever [underlined four times] so much for the check, but I don't need it as I get $1.00 a week and now that basketball training has started I have to swear off the Jigger until the season is over." "Jigger" probably referred to a now-obsolete golf club, an iron with low loft and short shaft. Irwin Miller was an enthusiastic golfer and in another letter, after describing the course in Watertown, wrote, "I can hardly wait to take some lessons when I get home. Clemy [Clementine] says that the course at home will be playable. I certainly hope so." The postscript read: "A week from today I will be on the St. Louisian [a train from the East Coast] 1 hr and 2 minutes from Indianapolis and the Packard!!!"[19]

In the fall of 1927, Irwin Miller and twenty-one of his Taft classmates (nearly half the class of forty-seven) headed thirty miles down the road to New Haven and Yale. Why Taft? Why Yale? Prestigious East Coast universities could be difficult for "western" students (an East Coast term for anyone west of the Alleghenies) who had not first gone to eastern prep schools.[20] Perhaps it was that geographical and social acclimation as much as any perceived academic weakness in Columbus high schools that accounted for Miller's being sent to Taft. After all, Clementine Miller was sent to Emma Willard in Troy, New York, before Smith College. Hugh Miller, Irwin Miller's father, had the scholarly background to appreciate the reputation of the nation's oldest and most respected universities. W. G. Irwin may have also heard favorable reviews about Yale through his business contacts in Indianapolis and New York. At that time, it was not uncommon for upper-class midwestern families to send their children to eastern boarding schools and colleges—consider Cole Porter (from Peru, Indiana, to Worcester Academy and Yale), F. Scott Fitzgerald (from St. Paul, Minnesota, to the Newman School and Princeton), and T. S. Eliot (from St. Louis to Milton Academy and Harvard).

At Yale, Miller majored in the classics and graduated Phi Beta Kappa in the class of 1931. There was not a lot of hanging out at Mory's with "gentlemen songsters, off on a spree" or anyone else. The tall, serious student from Indiana was still shy and modest about the family wealth, despite having a LaSalle roadster to drive around campus. Irwin would say later that he never quite adapted to the social side of collegiate life. "I just didn't know how to do it."[21]

Yale's president during Irwin Miller's years, James Rowland Angell, aimed for a more "intellectually oriented college," wrote one Yale historian. The result was "the emergence of a much more mature and sophisticated curriculum and the conversion of Yale into a university college—a place where the existence of art, music, graduate, and other schools added immeasurably to the undergraduate experience."[22] Wrote another, "While friendliness and organizing ability were at a premium, mere charm was not enough [for Yale]. Preparatory [school] men whose gifts were primarily social were supposedly instinctively to head for Harvard, Princeton, or Williams."[23]

Years later, when Irwin Miller led his hometown of Columbus, Indiana, to become a modern architectural showplace, people would try to pinpoint the origins of his interest in architecture. When Miller had given advice to the rest of the family about the architecture for a new building for their church, Elsie Sweeney would say that her nephew had taken an architectural appreciation course at Yale. Though there was a department of architecture at Yale (within the School of Fine Arts), the two relevant courses he officially took were an Introduction to Fine Arts and Modern English Painting. However, architectural theory and history may well have been a component of the Introduction course, which Miller took as a senior, since two of the professors who taught that course, Everett Victor Meeks and Shepherd Stevens, were architects by training.[24] During this period the modern movement was having a growing impact, and concepts in art and architectural education were changing, particularly under Dean Meeks, whom a colleague described as "a pioneer in the re-direction of architectural education in America in the 1920s."[25] Others suggested that since Eero Saarinen studied at Yale, this was the origin of Miller's interest in architecture. Not true, since the two passed like ships in the Yale-quadrangle night: Miller graduating in spring of 1931 and Saarinen enrolling in graduate school in the fall of 1931. The two would later become great friends, however, when Saarinen came to Columbus to assist his father, Eliel, with the spectacular but simple Tabernacle Christian Church.[26]

Great-uncle W. G. Irwin nixed graduate study at Harvard Business School after Yale, saying business could not be taught.[27] Irwin

Miller's father agreed, saying, as Miller told a later interviewer, "Business is more an art than a science. You ought to study the history and cultures of other countries and civilizations so that you can understand more deeply the society in which you will live and work."[28] Instead of going to Harvard, Miller headed for England and two years at Oxford (Balliol College), where he received a master's degree in political science, rowed, lost his stammer, and spent vacations traveling throughout Europe. He was *not* a Rhodes Scholar, he would carefully tell interviewers later: "People always think that an American who goes to Oxford must be a Rhodes Scholar. I wasn't."[29] While in England, he acquired a more intense appreciation of his surroundings. "In my whole life I know of no more powerful influence than the daily walk I had to take in Oxford from my college to the river and back, past Jesus College, down High Street, through Christ Church, Tom Quad, and the Long Walk, in every season, in every kind of weather," Miller told a National Convention of the American Institute of Architects many years later.[30]

In the summer of 1933, Miller returned to the United States, degree in hand and a head full of the sights and sounds of old and new Europe. By October he was in California working for Purity Stores, a large grocery chain in which the family had a substantial investment.[31] He was on the payroll at the company minimum of fourteen dollars a week, a positive example for the rest of the employees, even though Miller protested that he was also receiving money from the Irwin Estate in Columbus.[32] It was all part of W. G. Irwin's plan for easing Miller into the family's many commercial interests. "I still think the best place for you to begin is Purity Stores," W. G. Irwin had written Miller in May 1933. "When that is all over and you have been in the teller's cage at the Bank for a long enough period to know some of the people around here, I hope you will be ready to step in and see what can be done with the Starch Company and other things in which we are interested."[33]

FACING, Family patriarch Joseph I. Irwin was eighty-six years old when his great-grandson, Joseph Irwin Miller, was born. The baby's mother, Nettie Sweeney Miller, is on the left, and her mother, Linnie Irwin Sweeney, Joseph's daughter, is on the right. *Irwin-Sweeney-Miller Collection, Indiana Historical Society*

ABOVE, The ladies of the Irwin-Sweeney-Miller family were a formidable group. *Left to right*: Clementine Miller Tangeman, Nettie Sweeney Miller, Linnie Irwin Sweeney, Elsie Sweeney. *Irwin-Sweeney-Miller Collection, Indiana Historical Society*

ABOVE, Midwesterners Henry Ford and W. G. Irwin (*right*) built fortunes in the first half of twentieth-century America. *Irwin-Sweeney-Miller Collection, Indiana Historical Society*

FACING, Irwin Miller took up the violin at an early age and studied seriously throughout his life. His violin went with him when he went east to school. *Irwin-Sweeney-Miller Collection, Indiana Historical Society*

Cummins Corporate Office Building. Kevin Roche. 1984. *Carol M. Highsmith, Library of Congress*

5 Clessie

THE BIG PACKARD WITH THE FOUR-CYLINDER ENGINE SHOT OUT OF the converted barn behind the house on Fifth Street and into the alley—backward. By the time it had careened into the street, it had narrowly missed three trees and two fences. Nineteen-year-old Clessie Cummins had never even seen a Packard before, let alone driven one. But now that he was behind the wheel, he was not about to let that stop him from getting this new job as driver for banker W. G. Irwin, who was sitting in the passenger seat.

Because Cummins was small, he had trouble getting the big engine to turn over with the hand crank. Desperate, he tried a trick he had used with small boat engines. He dipped a rag in the gas tank, dripped a few drops of gas into the priming cups on each cylinder, and gently rocked the engine with the crank. It started. W. G. Irwin beamed. "'I'd rather have a man any time who can use his head instead of his back,' he shouted above the engine's roar." Clessie Cummins had the job.[1]

The family's previous chauffeur had been fired for lighting up a cigarette while driving. Now, in 1908, it would be Clessie Cummins who would drive assorted Irwins, Sweeneys, and Millers around town from spring through autumn. When winter arrived, the Packard went back up on blocks in the garage, and Cummins went back to work for the Marmon Motor Car Company in Indianapolis.

Clessie Cummins was cocky, friendly, ambitious, and a mechanical genius. He was born in 1888 in rural southern Indiana. As a young boy he loved to take apart mechanical things to see how they worked. However, unlike most boys who loved to tinker, he could generally put the metal objects lying in pieces all over the barn floor back together again. At the age of eleven, he carved wooden patterns for molds into which molten cast iron was poured to make parts for an engine to pump water on his father's farm.[2] His last year of schooling was the eighth grade.[3] He once said he stopped going because he knew more than they did. That might have been because "they" had made him take the eighth grade three times. And that might have been because the family moved often—twelve times before he had finished elementary school. His father's job as a manager of a company that made elm staves for barrels meant moving frequently to a fresh supply of elm trees. However, limited formal education in rural areas was not unusual at the time.

In the early 1900s, Indiana was the heart of America's fledgling automotive industry. By 1909 some thirty-six automobiles were being manufactured in the state. Cummins worked at two of these companies, American Motor Car Company and Marmon Motor Car Company, when he was not driving for W. G. Irwin.[4] It was a fortuitous time and place for a boy with an intellectual appetite for all things mechanical and the ability to absorb what he was seeing and learning. When Ray Harroun's yellow and black Marmon Wasp won the Speedway's first 500-Mile Race, Cummins was there, working in the pits.

In 1913, with W. G. Irwin advancing money for tools and a location, Cummins opened the Cummins Machine Works, an auto repair shop, first in an old decrepit Irwin building on Fifth Street and then in a section of the new garage behind the Irwin-Sweeney-Miller house.[5] Part of Cummins's obligation as tenant was to drive whenever the family needed him. W. G. Irwin never learned to drive. Cummins settled into a comfortable relationship with the family. Linnie Sweeney once said that hearing him whistling as he worked around the property reminded her nostalgically of her son Joe who had died.

A year after Cummins began to work for the family in 1908, baby Joseph Irwin Miller was born. Through the coming years, the young boy, as scion of the town's wealthiest family, had less freedom to traipse through town like other children. Instead, much of his time was spent hanging around the garage where Cummins tinkered and worked. The grown-up Cummins was markedly small—five feet six, only about 110 pounds—"I sometimes gave the impression of being an overgrown child," he would later explain.[6] Youthful wrestling matches and horseplay eventually ended as young Irwin Miller grew taller and stronger. Miller, however, would always consider Cummins his close friend.[7] In 1910, two years after going to work for the family, Cummins married Ethel McCoy, a reserved young woman who worked as a secretary for Z. T. Sweeney in his office above the garage.[8] The marriage lasted fifteen years until her death from influenza in the spring of 1925, a few weeks after the birth of their fifth child.[9]

With the growing involvement of the United States in World War I, automobile and bicycle repair at Cummins's company segued into full-time subcontract machine work for customers all over the state and beyond. W. G. Irwin helped by passing the word to many of his business contacts.[10] Locals chuckled at the time that W. G. Irwin, Linnie Sweeney, and the rest of the family arrived home from their annual summer trek to Canada and were astonished to find that Cummins had moved the family car into storage elsewhere and that the garage was filled with machines, a handful of employees, and piece parts for a war-related job for a local foundry.[11] Eventually Cummins moved the Cummins Machine Works to a building on Jackson Street that had once been a mill to make Cerealine, an early breakfast cereal.[12]

Clessie Cummins may have gotten his first look at an actual diesel engine sometime in 1915, when a small Hvid diesel was installed in a flour mill in Columbus. For some time Cummins had been reading about this new way of producing mechanical energy that carried the name of Rudolf Diesel, the German engineer who had obtained a patent for such an engine in 1892 and built a working prototype a year later.[13] Actually, an Englishman, Herbert Akroyd Stuart, had beaten Diesel in building such an engine by about two years,[14] and, even earlier, in nineteenth-century France, visionary scientists had written about this new kind of internal combustion engine. But Diesel continued to refine and develop his engine, whereas Akroyd Stuart did not do much after 1893 (which is why a century later the Columbus company would be known informally as Cummins Diesel and not Cummins Akroyd Stuart).

In basic terms, a diesel engine compresses intake air to a high pressure and uses the resulting high temperature to ignite the fuel. A gasoline engine, on the other hand, mixes air and fuel at relatively low temperature, then compresses this mixture that is ignited by a spark plug. Fuel to run a diesel could be of lower grade, hence cheaper. One gallon of diesel fuel (from crude oil) had 13 percent more energy than one gallon of gasoline (from crude oil).[15] Because diesel engines needed to be bigger and heavier, their use gradually gravitated to large machines—earth-moving equipment, railroad engines, and ships. As the Great War was winding down, diesel engines had powered both US Navy submarines and German U-boats.

The diesel design installed in the Columbus flour mill in 1915 had been developed by Rasmus M. Hvid, a Danish engineer who had become an American citizen.[16] At the time several American companies were producing these small engines under license to Hvid's company. In early January 1919, Cummins went to Chicago and signed an option for a license to manufacture a small Hvid diesel engine. The challenge then became financing. Manufacturing rights would cost $2,500 plus royalty of $5 per engine. W. G. Irwin agreed to put up the money to buy the license.

A month later on February 3, 1919, the Indiana secretary of state issued a certificate of incorporation for the Cummins Engine Company. Initial capitalization was $50,000: five hundred shares at $100 per share. W. G. Irwin received one hundred shares, and Cummins received two hundred shares in exchange for $20,000's worth of shop equipment. Thirty-one Columbus townspeople—lawyers, bankers, and store owners—took the remaining three hundred shares. Clessie Cummins was named president and one of five directors. At the first meeting of the directors at the offices of the chamber of commerce on the evening of February 21, 1919, William G. Irwin was elected to the board to replace a member who had resigned.[17]

Soon Cummins had patents pending for his own modifications to the diesel engine. (Some of these were assigned later to Hvid during negotiations to dissolve the Cummins contract with the Chicago-based company.)[18] But there were many frustrating complications in producing diesel engines and finding customers willing to give them a try—ups and downs, mostly downs—with W. G. Irwin putting more money into the fledgling company. Through the years there were tensions between the two, with W. G. saying on at least one occasion (according to Cummins), "I'm putting in money, and you are only putting in effort."[19] John R. Niven, a friend of both men and a Purity Store and Cummins executive said, "Clessie had many failures and disappointments, but the saving fact was that W. G. and Clessie never weakened at the same time."[20]

Cummins delighted in taking his diesel engines on the road and showing what they could do: a pitch to shrimp boat captains for marine diesels during an extended stay in Louisiana; a 792-mile trip from Indiana to New York City for the National Automobile Show in a diesel-powered Packard—on $1.38's worth of diesel fuel—which impressed the national media; a run in two Indianapolis 500-Mile Races in diesel-powered cars.[21]

W. G. and Clessie even took hulking car No. 8—the Cummins diesel-powered Duesenberg that had finished thirteenth in the 1931 Indianapolis 500—to Europe to demonstrate the engine's reliability and the relative "cleanliness" of its exhaust. Fitting out the racecar with a windshield and cloth roadster top, plus aluminum trunks for baggage mounted on the sides of the front, the two took off through the French countryside. While W. G. had visited Europe several times before, the 1932 trip was an eye-opener for Cummins. One evening on the ocean liner going over, Cummins sat at dinner (in first class) between General John J. Pershing and tennis star Helen Wills Moody. Once on land, W. G. made sure that Cummins's visit was about more than cars and engines. They visited Mont Saint-Michel, saw the Bayeux tapestry, visited the Louvre, the Arc de Triomphe, and Versailles and later, in Italy, saw Leonardo Da Vinci's *The Last Supper.*[22]

While W. G. and Clessie were waiting in Paris for a new Cummins Model H to be installed in a truck at the Citroen plant, they were joined by the ladies of the Irwin-Sweeney-Miller family, Linnie, Elsie, Nettie, and Clementine, who had been visiting Florence. While in Paris some of the ladies took Clessie shopping to buy dresses for his second wife, Estella (Stella), who was back in Columbus with the Cummins children.

Then it was off to Italy, Germany, and Switzerland for the men and No. 8. Stops along the way included a visit to a sprawling Fiat factory and laps on the company's high-banked, rooftop test track.[23] The two groups of travelers reunited again in England and visited their young relative, Irwin Miller, who was finishing his first year of graduate study in Oxford.

Several years earlier, thanks to arrangements made by W. G. Irwin, the ladies of the family had enjoyed their moment in the London sun—presentation at the Court of St. James's to King George V and Queen Mary. Linnie's presentation gown was lavender brocade, Elsie wore silver lamé, and Clementine's gown was matelassé (quilted) with a shoulder train. All wore the required three white feathers in their hair, the insignia of the Prince of Wales, as did the other two hundred or so women being presented that evening.

"Dear Unk," wrote twenty-three-year-old Clementine Miller, still dazzled the next day by the experience. She described walls paneled in ivory and gold leaf, mirrors everywhere, "flunkies who arranged your train for you," the lord chamberlain who shouted, "To be presented, Miss Clementine Miller," which, "miracle of miracles, he pronounced correctly," and curtsies as the king and queen exited to the strains of "God Save the King." "Thank you ever so much for making possible the greatest experience of my life. Lovingly and appreciatively, Clementine."[24]

❧ ❧ ❧

But for W. G. and Clessie, the emphasis on this 1932 trip was on engines. At the famous Brooklands racetrack outside London, the Cummins/Duesenberg No. 8 ran several sedate demonstration laps—sedate because Clessie was concerned about a piston seizing at high speed. A variety of engine problems had developed throughout the long trip, with Clessie scrambling to find parts and tools and make repairs.[25]

The trip, draining on both humans and racecar, had gathered much attention during the four-thousand-mile tour but no engine orders or license agreements. "The brief flurry of generated publicity unfortunately had done nothing to generate the financial resources needed in a time of severe economic conditions," Lyle Cummins, Clessie Cummins's son, would write many years later. Even Citroen, the most likely of customers, though pleased with the Model H engine's performance in its trucks, was nevertheless not in a financial position to continue the "promising venture."[26]

These "severe economic conditions" were just as serious in the United States. Like the rest of the country, Columbus was mired in the Great Depression. More than thirteen hundred banks in the United States had failed in 1930 alone, though the family's Irwin Union Trust Company in Columbus had survived.[27] A federal executive order temporarily closed the country's banks in early March 1933. The Columbus banks opened again without restriction on March 15. "The only thing we have to fear is fear itself," the country's new president, Franklin Delano Roosevelt (FDR), had told a nervous America in March 1933. Not that FDR's pithy aphorisms or the New Deal gave any comfort to W. G. Irwin, who had backed Republican president Calvin Coolidge and entertained Roosevelt's 1932 opponent Herbert Hoover at his home in Columbus. The Cummins Engine Company had not had a single year in the black, but economic conditions were improving slowly.

In 1934 Irwin Miller returned to Columbus from selling potatoes, stocking shelves, and learning about retail marketing in the Purity grocery chain in California. Despite some misgivings on the part of W. G. Irwin, who still wanted his great-nephew to start at the bank and "get to know people in town," Clessie thought it was time for Irwin to come to Cummins Engine Company. "I had a lot of responsibility in the bank when I was Irwin's age," W. G. Irwin had written to his sister Linnie, Irwin's grandmother. "I was not very much older than he is when the road [traction line] was built. . . . I can't see that his age would interfere."[28]

There was no point in having Irwin work his way up from the bottom, said Clessie, who was himself now vice president of the prestigious Society of Automotive Engineers. Besides, sitting in an office running a company was not Clessie's favorite thing to do. At the Cummins board of directors meeting in March 1935, twenty-five-year-old J. Irwin Miller was named vice president and general manager. The fascinating relationships between Clessie, Cummins, W. G. Irwin, and Irwin Miller—paradoxically both close and confrontational—would continue through the coming decades.

Clessie Cummins, a mechanical genius, was a country boy who first worked for the Irwin-Sweeney-Miller family as driver of their big Packard. He and his boss, banker W. G. Irwin, later teamed up to start the Cummins Engine Company. *Cummins Inc., Irwin-Sweeney-Miller Collection, Indiana Historical Society*

North Christian Church.
Eero Saarinen. 1964.
Balthazar Korab Archive, Library of Congress

6 Eliel and Eero

THE COLUMNED TEMPLES OF THE NILE VALLEY, THE GILDED DUOMOS of Venice, the great French cathedrals of the Middle Ages—through the centuries, religion has been the driving force behind audacious advances in architecture. In the late 1930s, it happened again, this time in the block between Fourth and Fifth Streets in Columbus, Indiana. Tabernacle Church of Christ had been the church (under different names) of W. G. Irwin's brother-in-law, the Reverend Zachary Taylor Sweeney, who had served as the church's popular minister from 1872 to 1898. Now with the congregation and Columbus's population growing, the church was too small.[1]

Not surprisingly, a new church building and the selection of an architect were frequent topics of conversation at the Irwin-Sweeney-Miller house. The current traditional redbrick church was just west of the family home on Fifth Street. W. G. Irwin and his sister, Linnie, gave land across the street (an entire city block) to the church as a new building site. The family was amply represented on the church building committee. Linnie Sweeney and her daughters Elsie and Nettie (Irwin's mother) were all members of the committee. The chairman was W. G. Irwin.

Irwin Miller, now back in Columbus after two years at Oxford and a year in California, heard and was part of the dinner table discussions concerning the new church. "Mother, I don't see why you talk about a Gothic Church or an Early American church—we are not Gothic or Early American," said Miller, his aunt Elsie recalled later. "My sister [Nettie] was somewhat alarmed at his line of thought as she knew he was referring to modern architecture, which she was not prepared to accept."[2]

However, other experts agreed that modern was the way to go. The first architect hired (the head of the Princeton School of Architecture) was unable to finish the commission because of poor health. The project stalled. Linnie Irwin Sweeney insisted her two daughters find an architect. "I want to see this church built before I die."[3] According to Elsie Sweeney, a member of the congregation knew of some recent, interesting work being done by an architect ("a Finn and his name begins with S") who was one of the leaders of the new Cranbrook Educational Community in Bloomfield Hills outside Detroit. His name was Eliel Saarinen.[4]

Eliel Saarinen, born in Finland in 1873, was the best-known graduate of the Helsinki Polytechnic Institute. He and several fellow young architects had built a common living and studio space overlooking a lake near Helsinki. It was in this rambling, thirty-eight-room house and studio that Eliel's son Eero was born August 20, 1910. This made Eero Saarinen a year younger and a contemporary of Irwin Miller, his eventual friend and patron.

With credit for the design of the impressive 1914 Helsinki Central Railway Station in his pocket and with post–World War I inflation and few major commissions on the horizon in Finland, Eliel Saarinen brought his family (including thirteen-year-old Eero) to the United States in 1922. He was lured by a *Chicago Tribune* architectural competition for a new *Tribune* office building (he won second prize of $20,000). A Detroit newspaper publisher, George G. Booth, and his wife, Ellen, a member of the Scripps newspaper clan, commissioned Saarinen to start a school, the Cranbrook Academy of Art, which would bring design concepts of prewar Finland to the fore. Some called Cranbrook the Scandinavian Bauhaus.

Cranbrook, like Frank Lloyd Wright's Taliesin East in Wisconsin, was considered an oasis of modern architectural thought by authors and critics. "Wright himself had a low opinion of Saarinen senior, characterizing him patronizingly as 'the best of the eclectics,'" wrote author Rupert Spade. "There was no contact between the two schools—except insofar as they formed stopping places for modern enthusiasts passing from west to east or vice versa."[5]

Eero Saarinen would later say he "practically grew up" under his father's drafting table, "and then when I was old enough to get on top, I was drawing on the other end of it."[6] Saarinen started studying sculpture and furniture design at Cranbrook, went on to study sculpture in Paris, and then headed for the Yale School of Architecture, where he spent three years and graduated with honors in 1934. After earning his degree, Saarinen won a traveling fellowship that allowed him to tour Europe, admiring old cityscapes and studying new architecture wherever he could find it. When he returned to the United States, Saarinen worked for a time for industrial designer Norman Bel Geddes and then with Charles Eames, whom he invited to come to Cranbrook and with whom he collaborated on advanced furniture design projects.[7] Eero Saarinen himself had returned to Cranbrook, where he met and married Lily Swann, who was studying ceramics at the school. He became an instructor of design and joined his father in working on several "challenging commissions,"[8] including a new, radically modern church being planned for a small town in southern Indiana.

Though there were already a few modern church buildings in the United States—a Frank Lloyd Wright Community Church in Kansas City and a few Catholic churches of contemporary design in New Jersey and elsewhere—this Columbus church, occupying an entire city block, would be the costliest modern church in the world. According to a later article in *Time*, putting the planned building into historical context, "Only in the past few years . . . has the Church moved to resume its ancient place as the patron of creative architecture."[9]

The Tabernacle Christian Church building committee had decided to contact Eliel Saarinen, a son of a Lutheran minister. He was not interested. Churches in the United States were too theatrical, he said—not his idea of religion.[10] Then Irwin Miller, the youngest member of the Miller family, tried again. In his letter Miller explained that this particular congregation believed in simplicity. Though money would not be a problem, the church was not interested in paying for luxury and display. The building committee's theme was "our church is our people." Miller's arguments, plus those from building committee members Elsie Sweeney and Nettie Miller, who visited Cranbrook, did the trick. Saarinen accepted the commission.[11]

The building committee in Columbus had supplied Eliel Saarinen with a lengthy and detailed description of what it hoped for in a new church building. In addition to reflecting simplicity of worship, physical features of the new church had to be in tune with the congregation's (and denomination's) beliefs and practices. At the front of the church there should be a large, enclosed baptistery (according to the denomination's practice, baptism was total immersion in a shallow pool, not just sprinkling with water). A Communion table should be in a central place of prominence.

"You may ask why we contemplate building a great church, why do we not spend the same money in Christian work and arrange to worship in less impressive surroundings," said the committee's memo to Saarinen. "A costly church can be justified, in our opinion, only so far as it inspires and stimulates people in living better lives. We are willing to pay for a church which is designed to achieve this end."[12] In their response, the architects showed that they had been listening carefully to their new clients. "When your fathers and mothers came from different corners of the old world and by various paths in the new [world] to form their communities in Indiana, they brought with them a variety of theological traditions, many of which were already obsolete," said the architects' statement. "In the effort to unite these different denominations into one that would be commonly acceptable, your fathers and mothers, instead of combining many sects, decided to go back to the fundamentals of Christian faith. From this decision, your church has emerged as a brotherhood of simple outer form and of rich inner life."

The architects then explained why the structure they proposed would be particularly appropriate. "As we compare this development of your church with that of the new architectural thought . . . we find that these are very much alike, . . . for as your church emancipated itself from theology, so the new architecture is endeavoring to build upon the fundamental principles of architecture."[13] With these careful explanations, the blueprints from the architects, which depicted a building that would be a radical departure from most new churches in the United States, were accepted unanimously by the congregation.[14] Earlier Nettie Miller, helped by Eero Saarinen, had talked Eliel Saarinen out of using the swastika as the emblem in the openings at the top of the bell tower. Saarinen senior argued that long before it had been usurped by the Nazis, the swastika had been a respected ancient symbol of life and motion in many cultures. Fortunately, he was persuaded to substitute the Jerusalem cross motif in the rows of openings at the top of the tower.[15]

Construction began in the fall of 1940, and the cornerstone was laid in April 1941 at a ceremony attended by an estimated 1,500 people.[16] War or no war, the handsome building with its simple but eloquent rectangular front with a grid of limestone panels and adjacent 166-foot freestanding bell tower was ready for dedication by the last Sunday in May 1942. Later that afternoon W. G. Irwin and his sister,

Linnie, who had together donated more than half the $750,000 cost of the complex, hosted a reception for the Saarinens at the family home across the street.

Eliel Saarinen's wife, Loja, was an important contributor to the new facility as well: she had led a team of weavers at Cranbrook who had created a tapestry that hung on the west wall at the front of the church depicting the Sermon on the Mount (Clementine's suggestion). It was said to be largest tapestry ever woven in the United States. The sanctuary where worship services would be held was bathed in white light from high, clear (not stained glass) windows and bleached oak pews. The church was structured as a complex of interconnected flat-roofed buildings containing a chapel, not one but two baptisteries, and meeting rooms and classrooms. Wings were connected to the main building by a two-story bridge and loggia, and more than half of the site was devoted to a sunken terrace containing a large reflecting pool (later filled in to become a sunken garden). Eero Saarinen may have collaborated with his father on the Columbus project, but the resulting structure was unmistakably Eliel Saarinen's in its "deliberate monumentality, use of water, and choice of materials," wrote architectural critic Allan Temko, citing particularly "the taut, freestanding campanile and noble nave" of the church. "Tabernacle Church of Christ in Columbus, Indiana (1940) . . . remains perhaps the purest exemplification of Eliel's longstanding dependence on contrasting horizontal and vertical forms," wrote Temko.[17] The asymmetrical arrangement of panels on the church's front and of the aisles in the main sanctuary were in keeping with one of the tenets of modernism.

The church and its furnishings garnered attention from the national press as well as the country's architectural media. *Newsweek* reported that during the first six weeks after the church's dedication nearly ten thousand visitors signed the church register. The church's architects had been "blessed with an almost unique combination of ample funds and an intelligent building committee," a later book (written, not surprisingly, by an architect) would point out.[18] This unbeatable combination of money and taste would be cited in the future when the success of Columbus architecture was analyzed. But just as important to Columbus was the friendship that developed between Irwin Miller and the Saarinens, particularly Eero. Both young, barely in their thirties, the two hit it off. In years to come, the Saarinen/Cranbrook network would bring other architects to Columbus to do some of their most daring and important early work.

Miller House, side terrace.
Eero Saarinen. 1957.
Balthazar Korab Archive, Library of Congress

7 Xenia

THE GIRL HAD ABILITY, NO QUESTION ABOUT IT. WHAT SHE NEEDED was opportunity, decided her Sunday school teachers, Clementine Miller and Nettie Sweeney Miller, Clementine's mother. The girl's name was Xenia Simons. Her father, a salesman for farm silos, had always liked the name of one of the towns in his territory, Xenia, Ohio—hence the name he gave his fourth and youngest child, born July 9, 1917, in Morgantown, Indiana, northeast of Columbus.[1]

Xenia, dark haired, bright, and ambitious, graduated from Columbus High School in 1934. Her father was struggling to make a go of a hickory furniture company, not an easy feat during the Depression. Nettie Miller offered to lend the girl money to go to business school, a loan that Xenia would repay with five dollars a week from her eight-dollar weekly salary at the Irwin Union Bank. She later moved on to a job at Cummins Engine Company, the fourteenth woman hired in the office. She continued to advance, learning as she went. After taking night classes in blueprint reading and metallurgy, she moved on from cataloging tools and engine parts to eventually becoming a buyer of castings. She joined the office union and became a member of the union's bargaining committee.

Things were improving slowly in the midst of the Depression. Songs on the radio told Americans that "Happy Days Are Here Again" and "Life Is Just a Bowl of Cherries." At Cummins Engine Company, if there weren't "Pennies from Heaven," at least there were more pennies. As the new general manager, J. Irwin Miller had continued to look, listen, ask questions, and learn. Reports he put together for W. G. Irwin showed the company's progress. In 1919 the Cummins plant employed fifteen men; in 1936 it employed approximately three hundred.[2] By 1934, some seven hundred out of eight hundred to one thousand diesel trucks in the United States were powered by Cummins engines.[3] A year later, in 1935, only 0.02 cents per dollar of sales were being lost, compared to $1.02 in 1932.[4] Even more significantly, net profit for the first quarter of 1937 was nearly $74,000 on gross sales of $807,000. It was the first time the company had shown a profit for more than one month, Miller reported to Irwin in March 1937.[5]

Meanwhile, as general manager Miller was involved in union activities as the company's workers struggled to decide upon representation. Chicago-based organizers from the Congress of Industrial Organizations (CIO), the federation of unions of skilled industrial workers, had been hungrily eyeing the company for some time.[6] In May 1937 Miller held a meeting of shopworkers at the high school auditorium. "You can join any organization you want or no organization. . . . So far you have been content to let us handle your affairs. Now the question is . . . whether you would do better to pay some gentlemen from Chicago to take over." The CIO lost out. The company's Independent Diesel Workers Union was formed in April 1938.

Miller had an interesting outlook toward unions from the beginning. Instead of antagonism, there was appreciation for unions from management. "I wouldn't know how to run a big company without a strong union," Irwin Miller would tell an interviewer from *Fortune* several years later. "The unions are management's mirror. They tell you things your own people won't admit."[7] As it turned out, another union meeting would turn out to be life altering for Miller in a way he likely never expected. At a meeting of the Cummins management and the company's office workers' union, the union bargaining committee was represented by a pretty young castings buyer, Xenia Simons. Miller and Simons began seeing one another after office hours—mostly "walks and talks," was the way Xenia would later describe it. Simons was perky and fun and had the confidence of knowing she was attractive to boys.[8] Miller was smitten. The slowly blossoming relationship between the boss and a girl in the office, though not exactly a secret, was kept out of sight of town gossips as much as possible, though they would sometimes be spotted walking to lunch together.

When they were not together, there were notes and long, affectionate, heartfelt, and often playful letters between "Gramma" and "Grampa," as they called one another. "Mr. Grandpop requests the pleasure of Miss Gramma's presence at lunch today—12.03—on account of he thinks she is wonderful," wrote Miller on a torn-out sheet from a desk calendar.[9] And another time, "I want to say to you over again of the things we talked about last night—how our love makes everything more loveable to me," he wrote. "People are nicer. Dogs more affectionate. Food tastes better than ever. I'll bet we're even immune to diseases."[10] Often the letters included charming stick-figure drawings.[11] Simons responded in kind. "Grampa, don't let's let little things come between us. We are the most important thing, or rather our love for each other should come above everything."[12]

The letters between the young lovers in Columbus contained serious discussions as well. In the early 1940s, the world beyond Columbus, beyond Indiana, beyond the United States, was convulsing. Germany and its Axis allies were grabbing new territory in Europe and the Pacific. In December 1941 Japan bombed the US naval base at Pearl Harbor, Hawaii, and the United States became well and truly committed to World War II.

Cummins Engine Company had already been involved in limited war-focused activities. One morning in October 1941, Columbus residents had been astonished to see a light tank rumble down Fifth

Street on the way from the plant to the train station to be shipped to the Aberdeen Proving Grounds. Powering it was a Model HBS supercharged truck engine, replacing earlier unsatisfactory engines made elsewhere. Clessie Cummins was at the controls, his brother Don Cummins was in the turret, and Miller was riding inside.[13]

All over the country, young men were signing up to serve. Thirty-two year-old Irwin Miller received a naval reserve commission in August 1942. Before he left, Miller prepared his will—miscellaneous shares of stock to Simons and to Maynard Mack, his Taft and Yale pal, and the rest to his sister Clementine Miller.[14]

"There is only one thing about C-E-Co [Cummins Engine Co.] that bothers me in leaving, Gramma," he wrote to Simons. The "spirit" at Cummins "is a treasure without price, and it can be so easily lost. If we become hard of heart, we shall lose it. If we become thoughtless of individuals, we shall lose it. If we lose our ability to feel sorry, we shall lose it. If we lose our humility we shall lose it. . . . We cannot leave this all to chance," he continued earnestly. "We must study to perfect ourselves in the art of harmonious cooperation. We must learn those things that inhibit it; and we must become masters of those things which foster it." And because Simons was also at Cummins, she would understand what he was driving at. "There is no one who understands and feels all this so well as you, my sweet. It is so easy to write it to you where it would be near impossible to say it to another."[15]

After several months of basic training, Lieutenant Miller was sent off to Washington to await his posting at sea. Clessie Cummins was now also in Washington, working as diesel production director for the War Production Board as a "dollar-a-year" man. Miller asked his old friend for advice about whether to marry before shipping out. Cummins said yes, if he truly loved the girl.[16] At some point Miller had also discussed marriage with W. G. Irwin. His great-uncle had "rather strongly" advised him to get married, Miller remembered many years later in his journal. "He told me that he failed to get married 'out of laziness.'"[17]

The family back in Columbus assumed—preferred—the pair would wait until after the war. But war was changing many romantic timetables. Simons headed east and the two married in a small Washington-area chapel in February 1943. Their only attendants were Clessie Cummins and his wife Stella, though W. G. Irwin came to visit the newlyweds in their Arlington apartment shortly afterward.[18]

This period illustrated dramatically the Gordian knot of complications in the relationships between Clessie Cummins and the Irwin-Sweeney-Miller family. The wedding at which Cummins had been Miller's best man was in February. Yet only five months earlier, a lengthy memo showed Cummins's still bitter unhappiness with his treatment in a company restructuring a year earlier.[19] There seemed to be a genuine difference in opinion between W. G. Irwin and Cummins about the relative importance of capital, which Irwin provided (as much as $2.25 million by 1936), and the ideas, inventions, and labor that Cummins provided. In many ways it was a classic economic clash.[20] Yet Irwin was proud of Cummins. He was proud, for instance, when Cummins, "a man whose education in the schools ended in the 8th grade," was invited to go to Boston to address a major meeting of the New England Engineering Societies.[21]

"To me the whole situation is tragic," wrote Cummins in that 1942 memo. "My life's work and the future of a worthwhile enterprise is being wrecked. For what—slavery to the idea that only money can have its wages guaranteed." But Miller, he said in the same memo, "is still my pal and almost my son."[22]

Elsewhere, there was a war going on. Lieutenant Joseph Irwin Miller received orders to report to the aircraft carrier USS *Langley*, which was heading for action against the Japanese in the Pacific.

Xenia Simons, a local Columbus girl, met J. Irwin Miller when he returned to Columbus to join the family businesses. *Irwin-Sweeney-Miller Collection, Indiana Historical Society*

During World War II, with Navy Lt. Irwin Miller's ship due to depart for the Pacific, Xenia Simons traveled east so the two could be married.
Irwin-Sweeney-Miller Collection, Indiana Historical Society

While in Washington, Irwin's great-uncle, W. G. Irwin, visited the newlyweds in their Arlington, Virginia, apartment. *Irwin-Sweeney-Miller Collection, Indiana Historical Society*

As an executive officer aboard the light aircraft carrier USS *Langley*, Irwin Miller (*back row, center*) saw action in battles for the Marshall Islands, northeast of Australia. *Irwin-Sweeney-Miller Collection, Indiana Historical Society*

Irwin Union Bank, now
Irwin Conference Center.
Eero Saarinen. 1954.
Balthazar Korab Archive, Library of Congress

8 Home

CARRYING 1,569 MEN, INCLUDING EXECUTIVE OFFICER LT. IRWIN Miller, the light aircraft carrier USS *Langley* left Philadelphia in early December 1943, heading for Pearl Harbor, then on to support the landing of American forces on the Japanese-held Marshall Islands, northeast of Australia.[1]

Meanwhile, Xenia Miller had headed back home to Columbus to stay with friends and await the birth of their first child. Margaret Irwin Miller was born on December 12, 1943, at a hospital up in Indianapolis. Her dad did not receive word until after his ship had left Honolulu. Once mother and baby were back in Columbus, the baby's grandfather, Hugh Miller, made it a practice to stop by to see the newest member of the family in the evening on his way home from his office at the bank.

Other news from Indiana for Irwin, aboard ship in the Pacific, was not so good. W. G. Irwin, who had been on the board of the Indiana National Bank in Indianapolis since 1921, had been elected president of this, the state's largest bank, in early 1942. He generally spent two days a week up in his Indianapolis office.

On December 14, 1943, while passing through the marble lobby of the Indianapolis bank, W. G. collapsed from a heart attack and died.

He had turned 77 a month earlier and was known to have heart problems. Just that morning before leaving Columbus, he had received a letter from Clessie resigning as Cummins president. It had upset him greatly, reported his niece Nettie, who had driven him to his office in Indianapolis.

Among the paradoxical aspects of Clessie's bitter letter was that it was written only ten months after the happy occasion of Clessie and Stella's participation in Irwin and Xenia's wedding, but then Clessie had always seemed able to keep his affection for Irwin separate from his sporadic flashes of anger at what he saw as his mistreatment by the company that bore his name. After W. G.'s death, Clessie withdrew his resignation request. Another family death followed less than two months later, that of Linnie Irwin Sweeney, W. G.'s sister and Irwin's grandmother.

The news reached Irwin in the central Pacific where the *Langley* had moved on to the battles for New Guinea and the formidable Japanese naval base at Truk. There the *Langley* and her planes destroyed or damaged some thirty-five Japanese planes while losing only one aircraft.[2] It was on the *Langley*, "as a deck officer maneuvering an aircraft carrier" through battles, that Irwin Miller "learned he could hold his own in an outfit his family did not own," said a later article in *Fortune*.[3]

Irwin applied for leave to return home to help the family cope and to assist with the stability of Cummins Engine Company's crucially important wartime engine production. A ninety-day leave was converted into permanent release from duty, and Irwin was elected executive vice-president of Cummins in 1944. He asked Clessie to stay on as president.

In May of 1947, Irwin's father, Hugh Thomas Miller, died at the age of 80. Irwin remembered him as someone who loved learning all his life and often recalled his advice that business was more an art than a science. His father had advised him, "You ought to study the history and cultures of other countries and civilizations so that you can understand more deeply the society in which you will live and work."[4]

Upon his father's death, Irwin took over operation of the family bank. A full plate indeed, since two years earlier Irwin had moved up to president of Cummins, when Clessie at last made good on his plan to move to California. (In 1951 Clessie would ask to be totally released from his obligations to the company.)

Clementine, who had served with the Red Cross in Europe during the war, had astonished the family by deciding to marry at the age of 46. The groom was an old friend, Dr. Robert Stone Tangeman, an accomplished pianist with a special interest in liturgical music. He had first known the family through Aunt Elsie when he taught at the Indiana University School of Music, and Elsie, herself a serious amateur pianist, served as a patron of the music school. Among his more impressive credits was that when noted pianist Nadia Boulanger, with whom he had studied in Paris, visited Indiana University and Bloomington in 1944, the two performed the world premier of Igor Stravinsky's "Sonata for Two Pianos."[5]

After the war, when Clementine moved to New York to work for the national and international Girl Scouts, their friendship had been rekindled, since Bob Tangeman, now divorced, was teaching at Juilliard and Union Theological Seminary. The two were wed in a surprise ceremony at the family home on Fifth Street in Columbus on Thanksgiving Day, 1951, and Clementine acquired a 15-year-old stepson, John Tangeman. The day was also (no accident) a day honoring St. Cecilla, the patron saint of music.

But some things did not change, for instance the family's annual summer trek to the Muskoka lake country in Canada. With a growing family of three lively little girls—in addition to Margaret, there were Catherine (Kitty) born in 1946, and Elizabeth (Betsey) born in 1948—Irwin and Xenia, with a polite nudge from the older generation, agreed it was time to build their own separate house in the family compound. Irwin contacted his old friend Eero Saarinen, who designed for them a modern structure perched on a rock overlooking Lake Rosseau. Using natural woods found in the area, it would not have looked out of place in the north woods of Finland. It was christened Llanrwst, in keeping with the practice of using Welsh names for houses on the property.

Irwin had another commission for Eero back in Columbus—a new facility for the Irwin Union Bank. The resulting flat-roofed, glass-walled building, with street setbacks for trees and flower beds, again brought attention from the national architectural press to the little town in southern Indiana. "The bank's newest home, on the corner right across from the old one, sums up some striking changes in the art of banking," wrote *Architectural Forum*. "The vault is still secure, in the basement, but the proud impregnable façade has become a bright open pavilion, kept lower than its neighbors and opening up a little square where the town most needs light, greenery and change of pace." The roof was topped with nine opaque domes of shell concrete, leading some local wags to refer to it as the "brassiere factory."[6] The floor was a practical basket-weave brick, since Miller wanted to make sure a farmer or a factory worker with dirt or oil on his boots would not feel out of place walking in to do business.[7] Landscape architect Dan Kiley had worked with Eero on this verdant, downtown "change of pace."[8]

The bank was intentionally kept low, explained Saarinen in a series of oral interviews a year later. "The total environment is always more important than the individual building, and that's why when we built this medium sized bank in the little town of Columbus, Indiana, our big concern was how to put a building [so as] not to hurt but to help the town." The challenge, he said, was "to respect the integrity of the town and also to build an uncompromisingly modern building."[9]

Marvin Mass was a systems engineer who was involved in Columbus from the late 1950s to the 1980s. The New York firm he headed (Cosentini) took care of the unglamorous but necessary stuff—the heating and air conditioning and other mechanical systems. Among the Columbus buildings for which Mass's firm did the engineering were the Irwin Union Bank, North Christian Church, the Cummins Engine Plant (and one in the UK), the Columbus Post Office, and the Hamilton Center Ice Arena.

His work with architects gave him a chance to observe them at close range. He was particularly impressed by Eero Saarinen. "Saarinen was the most unassuming great man I've ever met," he said in his memoir, *The Invisible Architect*. "Not only did he solicit his staff's ideas," but he was willing to give them credit. Saarinen gave his associates Kevin Roche and John Dinkaloo "the freedom and authority they needed, so that when he died, the firm continued. That kind of behavior is unusual among 'star' architects."[10]

Landscape architect Dan Kiley's contributions were particularly visible in the dramatic setting for the new house Eero Saarinen was building for Xenia and Irwin on thirteen acres of farmland on the north side of town. A fourth child, a son, Hugh Thomas Miller II, had been born in 1951. A fifth child, William Irwin, would be born in 1956 while the house was under construction. No longer would the traditional two-story, white-painted brick house with dark shutters where they had been living provide sufficient space for the growing family—or suit Irwin and Xenia's increased interest in contemporary architecture and design.

Two others were important collaborators on the landmark house, Eero's chief associate, the Irish-born architect Kevin Roche, and the architect and interior designer Alexander Girard. One of the first challenges was where to place the house, since some of the land was in the flood plain of the Flatrock River. Xenia took a look at where Eero had at first positioned the house and reminded him that in times of floods she would have to transport the children to school by boat. The house was moved to higher ground.[11]

Xenia's eye was gradually being trained by designer Girard as they searched for the right furnishings for the new house. They might be in an antique store, for instance, and he would tell her to pick out the three best things in the shop.[12] (It was a technique Xenia and Irwin would later use on museum trips with their own children.) Girard loved bright colors and folk art, and collectibles and fabrics in the house reflected this. This new knowledge of art and design built upon the skills Xenia already had from her Cummins days of being able to read blueprints and other technical drawings. This made her well able to be involved as plans for the innovative new house moved forward.

One of the most distinctive features in the house was a large conversation pit in the open living room, a feature that would mark the house as a design of its time (the 1950s), as a museum curator would point out later.[13] It was Alexander Girard's idea.[14] The brilliant fuchsias, pinks, and corals of the fabrics on the pit's long cushions and nests of plump pillows would be changed with the seasons. And because the sunken area was five steps down from the surrounding living room, views through the house's walls of windows—of masses of wildly colorful blooms and immaculate trimmed hedges—were never obscured. Even the underside of the six-foot-eleven-inch Steinway Model B grand piano was painted scarlet red since it was visible from the lower conversation pit.[15]

The Miller children relished the pit and the house's wide porches for a different reason. Will and visiting pals delighted in turning flips down into the pit's soft cushions. The girls found the wide terrace surrounding the house perfect for roller skating. "My sisters and I would grab on to the poles and twirl around," Margaret would remember later. "It would create a tremendous racket. Our parents were very tolerant."

Four separate living areas extended from the central living and dining rooms: the master bedroom suite; the children's area, with small bedrooms and a central study and play room; a guest suite; and a service area with kitchen and breakfast area. For more formal dining there was Saarinen's large round dining table in an area adjacent to the open living room. In its center was a recessed shallow pool in which flowers could be floated for dinner parties.

A half-century later, the Miller house would be called one of the five most significant mid-century modern houses still existing in the United States.[16]

Schmitt School.
Harry Weese. 1957.
Don Nissen,
Columbus Visitors Center

9 Harry

IN THE FALL OF 1950, IRWIN MILLER AND THE MAYOR OF COLUMBUS, Robert Stevenson, arrived at the small Michigan Avenue office of Chicago architect Harry Weese. As it turned out, it was a significant meeting for all three men—and the beginning of the architectural adventure on which Columbus was about to embark.

Weese had to rustle up chairs for his two tall visitors, one of whom he thought looked like Abraham Lincoln (Stevenson).[1] The two visitors were interviewing architects in several cities in the area to find the right person to design new housing for downtown Columbus. Weese had been recommended by Eero Saarinen, who had known him at Cranbrook. Weese perched on a stool, listened to his visitors, and spoke of his ideas of standardized buildings, refined during his graduate studies at Massachusetts Institute of Technology (MIT).[2] Miller was impressed to find a "very complete" presentation from Weese on his desk when he returned to Columbus.[3] Weese was also impressed by Miller and the "remarkable town" of Columbus, as he reported in a letter to Eero Saarinen. "I . . . congratulate you on your choice of client."[4]

With the war over, industries across the United States, including Cummins, were pushing to meet pent-up demands. New employees meant new young families who needed affordable but well-built housing. There was no appropriate rental housing in the town. "The bright young graduates of Wharton or Harvard Business School would come to Columbus and live for a while, maybe a year to get their feet on the ground and decide whether they wanted to buy a house or what kind of housing they wanted," Weese explained later.[5] This demand led to the construction of Harry Weese's Columbus Village Apartments on Twenty-Eighth Street, a few blocks east of the courthouse; the first phase was completed in 1953.[6] Next Weese designed a couple of homes in town and then, in 1957, most significant of all, the first of the eye-popping new public schools to be part of the Cummins Foundation Architectural Program. The Lillian C. Schmitt Elementary School (named for a longtime, respected Columbus teacher) was scaled to feel familiar to young children and had an interesting zigzag roofline, almost like a line of small houses.

Weese had a reputation as a fast and prolific designer (facetiously it was said that he could design a building in fifteen minutes). Other architectural historians have pointed out that he was a "first-strike" designer—he didn't go over lines twice.[7] "Harry's buildings never beat their chests or stood on their hands in an effort to dazzle. They simply answered the needs of body and soul," wrote author, architect, and photographer Balthazar Korab.[8] Weese would eventually be involved in the design of eighteen projects in Columbus, ranging from a beloved skating rink to bank branches, more schools, and a golf course clubhouse. His later spectacularly simple brick and slate First Baptist Church (1965), in a setting designed by landscape architect Dan Kiley, would be considered by some the most beautiful blossom in the Columbus bouquet of modernist buildings. Kiley and Weese worked well together, wrote Robert Bruegmann, Weese's biographer. "Both favored a direct, modern approach to design, grasping a problem as a whole, laying out the entire scheme, and then entrusting younger members of the office with the task of working out the details."[9]

Irwin Miller also trusted young talent. With the help of his friend Saarinen, working with Pietro Belluschi, the modernist head of the MIT School of Architecture, a short list was put together of possible architects to design Columbus public schools. Many were in the early stages of their careers. (For instance, the first segment of Weese's landmark Washington Metro project would not open until 1976.)[10] If the school board chose an architect from the list, the Cummins Foundation would pay the architectural fees for designing the school.[11] Irwin explained his thinking and the evolution of this remarkable civic project in carefully reasoned notes, possibly for a speech to the school board,[12] written in blue ink on lined school paper in an erect, legible script, half written, half printed. Major ideas were underlined in red ink or enclosed within neatly drawn red boxes. It is as if the wheels in Miller's mind could be seen turning.

Cummins Engine Company, he explained, competed successfully in the increasingly global diesel engine business, not in dollars—"GM would beat us"—but in the quality of its people. "The hardest job of all in business is to attract and hold outstanding people [encased in a red box]." And why was this so hard? "Because such people can choose for whom they work and where to live." Generally speaking, he continued, such people are highly educated and have many interests. Columbus has a hard time competing with big cities and other parts of the country—"California and recreation, New England and culture." But good families are "interested above all in their children [red box within a red box]. They know that more than in the past, a child's chance to compete in the future will depend on the amount and quality of education." The big question that the kind of people Cummins wanted to hire would be asking themselves, continued Miller, was, "If my boy or girl is able and wants to, will he have as good a chance at quality education—high school and beyond—at Columbus as in other communities?"

And after discussing inflation, taxes, and the fact that spending money now would save money for taxpayers over the long run, Miller moved on to the central core of the presentation. "We [Cummins Engine Foundation] favor and will support an aggressive, and intelligently conceived building program." Buildings, he admitted, are only part of a quality school system. "Teachers and curriculum are of equal or greater importance," but "buildings can help [red box]." He continued, "Buildings can support or impede the teacher. Buildings can make schooling a pleasant memory for children—or unpleasant." By the time of Lady Bird Johnson's visit in the fall of 1967, five elementary schools and a middle school had been designed with support from the Cummins Foundation. The younger children of Irwin and Xenia Miller were among the Columbus children trooping each morning into these and the half-dozen schools that would follow.

Other matters were occupying Irwin Miller in the 1950s and '60s. He now walked with a slight limp, after a not-much-discussed bout with polio in the late 1940s. But for the most part, his participation in physical activities did not seem to be much affected—he was still able to go ice skating and horseback riding with his children, for instance. "He was lots of fun," eldest daughter Margaret remembered. "He was good with kids," she said, "and would volunteer every year at the school carnival. My friends loved him."[13]

And his limp did not affect his love for golf. Prolific golf course designer Robert Trent Jones was hired (by the Cummins Foundation Architecture Program) to design a public eighteen-hole, 7,258-yard golf course in the gently rolling countryside five miles east of Columbus. (Jones's son later designed an additional nine holes.)[14] Otter Creek, which meandered through the property, was the name given to the new golf club, with a clubhouse designed by Harry Weese and Dan Kiley. Irwin Miller spoke at the dedication of Otter Creek in June 1964. His 326-word address, posted in the clubhouse, would become much quoted for explaining not only why a company would give a state-of-the-art golf course to the public, but also for what it revealed about Miller's general philosophy toward his community.

> Why should an industrial company organized for profit think it a good and right thing to take a million dollars and more of that profit and give it to this community in the form of this golf course and club house? Why instead isn't Cummins—the largest taxpayer in the county—spending the same energy to try to get its taxes reduced, the cost of education cut, the cost of city government cut, less money spent on streets and utilities and schools?
>
> The answer is that we should like to see this community come to be not the cheapest community in America, but the best community of its size in the country. We would like to see it become the city in which the smartest, the ablest, the best young families anywhere should like to live . . . a community that is open in every single respect to persons of every color and opinion that makes them feel welcome and at home here . . . a community which will offer their children the best education available anywhere . . . a community of strong, outspoken churches of genuine cultural interests, exciting opportunities for recreation . . . a community whose citizens are themselves well-paid and who will not tolerate poverty for others, or slums in their midst.
>
> No such community can be built without citizens determined to make their community best, without city government which works boldly—ahead of its problems, and not always struggling to catch up—and without money sufficient to get the job done.
>
> So Cummins is not for cheap education, or inadequate, poorly-paid government, or second-rate facilities or low taxes just for the sake of low taxes. Our concern is to help get the most for our dollar to help build this community into the best in the nation. And we are happy to pay our share, whether in work, or in taxes, or in gifts like this one.

One of the most spectacular of Harry Weese's houses for the Miller family—or for anyone—was not in Columbus but in Canada in the family's beloved Muskoka compound. (Weese also had remodeled a cottage that was called the Birdcage and designed a boathouse with flower boxes and a tall, heart-pounding waterslide.) This new house, for Clementine Miller Tangeman and her husband, Robert, was perched on a small rocky island in Lake Rosseau, just offshore from the other family dwellings. The house was close enough, but private and independent, like Clementine herself. It could only be reached by boat (or for hardier visitors, a quick swim from the mainland). Weese designed a small electric, double-ended ferry that looked like a toy tug boat. It docked at the boathouse tower with an elevator that took family and visitors thirty-five feet to the house's main floor. The Weese house for the Tangemans at Muskoka was all glass, natural woods, and dramatically angled rooflines set among towering pine, hemlock, and birch trees. Not surprisingly, a grand piano was among its furnishings. Following tradition, it was given a Welsh name, Llanfair.[15]

❧ ❧ ❧

In 1955 *Fortune* magazine embarked on a new project to publish an annual list of the five hundred leading US companies, ranked by annual revenue. Cummins Engine Company made the first list of the *Fortune* 500, coming in at 434. Another Columbus company, Arvin Industries, maker of automotive components, also made the list at 474. Not too bad for a rural town with a population of fewer than twenty thousand. Two years later, in 1957, the first public offering was made of Cummins stock from one-third of the family's holdings.

Though there were the inevitable ups and downs, under Irwin Miller's leadership the company grew and prospered. In 1955 Cummins had revenues of $59.2 million and 2,850 employees. By 1960 Cummins, which now led the field in heavy truck diesels, had revenues of $147 million and 6,118 employees.[16] After five years as president, Miller had become chairman of the board in 1951, and Robert Huthsteiner, an MIT graduate who had joined the company in 1942, was named president. This not only broadened the corporate governance but also gave Miller freedom from the day-to-day running of the company. Huthsteiner served for nine years before Don Tull, a homegrown Columbus boy who started on the shop floor, took over in 1960.

Cummins might be prospering, but elsewhere in town there were shadows—specifically within the Tabernacle Church of Christ, the Eliel Saarinen landmark masterpiece on Fifth Street. Tabernacle's doctrine and governance were growing increasingly conservative. Women, for instance, were expected to take a supportive, non-leadership role in church affairs. Conflict occurred between new biblical scholarship and conservative church teachings, explained Richard D. N. Dickinson, president of Christian Theological Seminary in Indianapolis and longtime friend of the Miller family. Irwin Miller's beliefs were not stuck in the conservative past. He was interested in the new biblical scholarship and in new ways of looking at his faith. Wrote Dickinson, "Miller was always probing the implications of basic gospel ethics."[17] There also may have been reluctance from conservative leaders of Tabernacle to embrace a more ecumenical Christianity.[18] Irwin Miller himself believed in Christian unity and would serve from 1960 to 1963 as president of the ecumenical National Council of Churches, the first non-clergyman to hold that position.

In 1955 nearly fifty members of the congregation, including Irwin Miller and other members of the Irwin-Sweeney-Miller family, decided to leave Tabernacle Church.[19] Church splits are always painful. For Miller, whose life would always be undergirded by his religion and whose family had been part of the Tabernacle Church for four generations, this must have been particularly true. He would never publicly discuss details of the falling out. With the death of Z. T. and Linnie Sweeney, their daughter Elsie, Irwin Miller's aunt, was said to be the family's spiritual head. Yet Elsie, too, was troubled by Tabernacle's "unwillingness to acknowledge the full Christian status of people in other churches who had been baptized in a way other than the Disciples' mode."[20]

In 1957 Tabernacle changed its name to First Christian Church. Then in 1963 the breakaway group moved into Eero Saarinen's new six-sided North Christian Church, its 192-foot spire piercing the sky like a giant's—or God's—needle.

Attitudes at the Disciples of Christ Seminary at Butler University's School of Religion in Indianapolis were at this point more in line with the expansive and inclusive beliefs of Irwin Miller and Elsie Sweeney than those at their former church had been. For several generations, Irwins, Sweeneys, and Millers had been deeply involved with Butler's School of Religion. When the Disciples of Christ Seminary decided it was time to become independent of its Butler University roots, Irwin, Xenia, and Clementine Miller all helped provide financing and played important roles in building its new home. Eero Saarinen had been chosen as architect for the school, now known as Christian Theological Seminary (CTS). When Saarinen's drafting table full of commitments precluded his taking on the commission, the commission went to another of the country's young architects, Edward Larrabee Barnes, among those whom Saarinen recommended. Building on a spectacular site in northwest Indianapolis overlooking the White River, Barnes described his design as "pre-Gothic." With its plain, geometric forms and simple surfaces, the new building would have "an affinity with the Middle East and the time of Christ," explained the architect.[21] Barnes would also design the W. D. Richards Elementary School in Columbus, where the saw-toothed roofline with skylights was said to be inspired by the look of early factories in the industrial Midwest.

Irwin Miller, as first chairman of the board of CTS, spoke at the ground breaking in March 1964 (construction would not be completed for another two years). Miller emphasized some familiar themes. Christian Theological Seminary historian Keith Watkins wrote that Miller explained why money should be spent on expensive buildings in a world of hardship by saying "one of the great purposes of education is to bring to each generation the best that the previous generations have accomplished."[22] And then Miller used one of his favorite quotations, this time from Winston Churchill: "We shape our buildings, and then they shape us."

In keeping with his beliefs in ecumenical Christianity, Miller, as head of the National Council of Churches, was also serving on the executive committee of the World Council of Churches (WCC). One of the World Council's challenges was bringing the Russian Orthodox Church into the organization. This involved several trips to the Soviet Union, with delegations that included, at various times, Irwin Miller; Episcopal bishop Henry Sherrill, like Miller a member of the Yale Corporation Board; and activist protestant leader Dr. Eugene Carson Blake.

Blake was impressed by Miller, who was one of his supporters on the WCC. On one trip to Russia, Miller shared his experience talking to the press with others on the trip who had not had as much experience either with the press or in Russia. Reporters, naturally, would be interested in the strength of the church in Russia. According to Blake, Miller pointed out that "newsmen" don't like you to say "no comment" when they ask you a question.

> "The thing to do is to make a brief speech on a closely related subject," said Miller. "Let me illustrate. I was asked if it wasn't true that most of the people in the Russian churches were old women. Of course, that was true. It's true in New York, too. But that's another subject. But if you say 'Yes'," Miller continued, "that's what they wanted from you, but you don't say that. You say, 'You know, I've been in Russia for two weeks now, and I've never been to church so many times in my life—mornings, evenings, weekdays, Sundays, every time. And one interesting thing: I've not been in one church that there hasn't been young people in it.'" And that was his headline.[23]

On one occasion the WCC delegation visited Yaroslavl, an ancient city on the Volga River northeast of Moscow, where winter temperatures could get down to thirty or forty degrees below zero. Among the manufacturing facilities in the modern city of Yaroslavl was a diesel engine plant. Miller took the opportunity to ask the plant's director if they had found any way to start diesel engines in cold weather. "No way but the old way," the Russian replied. "Light a fire under them."[24]

First Baptist Church.
Harry Weese. 1965.
Don Nissen, Columbus Visitors Center

10 JFK, LBJ, JIM

THE MAGISTERIAL, GOLD-AND-WHITE EAST ROOM OF THE WHITE House was filling up quickly. Chairs moved quietly on the gleaming oak parquet floor as some 250 national religious leaders settled into their seats on Monday afternoon, June 17, 1963. Irwin Miller, as president of the National Council of Churches, had flown in on Cummins's Sabreliner 265C for this meeting of the president's special commission on religion and race. President John F. Kennedy had asked Miller to chair the meeting and oversee follow-up actions.[1] The meeting, originally planned for approximately one hundred upper-echelon religious leaders of all faiths, had been buffeted by jealousies and turf protection in the growing civil rights movement—"the babble of voices," as one author called it.[2] The size of the final invitation list had produced delays in admission at the Pennsylvania Avenue White House gates and general dissatisfaction over the lack of personal contact with the president. Martin Luther King Jr., anxious to have a private meeting with Kennedy, had been invited to the Monday meeting but had canceled abruptly after finding out he would be only one among several hundred attending.[3]

The president intended to introduce his first major piece of civil rights legislation to Congress in a few days, and this was one of a series of meetings to gauge the support the legislation could expect from special interest groups. Dramatic events in the South—demonstrators being beaten and facing water hoses and police dogs—had been broadcast on the evening news and horrified audiences all over the country. Kennedy had been drawn more completely into the battle. He had stunned his advisors by deciding to address the nation on television about civil rights on June 9. And then a new tragedy. Just hours after Kennedy's TV address, NAACP activist Medgar Evers was murdered as he entered his house in Jackson, Mississippi.

This June 17 White House meeting a week later was brief. Kennedy announced that J. Irwin Miller would be chairman of the continuation of the president's special committee. White House staff promised that more meetings would follow, and Miller returned to Washington three days later to meet with the president's civil rights assistants. All that resulted, however, was an ambitious list of sixteen objectives and actions for the country's religious community. Sample suggested actions included the following:

- "In each community form and participate actively in a bi-racial committee which includes a cross-section of the community."
- "Urge individuals in each city to appear publicly with members of his opposite race at restaurants, theatres, athletic contests, etc."

Sample objectives were more ambitious:

- "Desegregation of privately owned public facilities (restaurants, theatres, rest rooms, hotels, lunch counters, etc.)."
- "Desegregation of congregations."
- "Additional non-menial employment for Negroes."
- "Desegregation of public schools and other state and municipal facilities (e.g. parks, libraries)."[4]

Miller responded to Washington immediately: "We are proceeding as rapidly as possible to activate the continuation committee."[5]

Two months later in Indianapolis, in the early morning hours of Wednesday, August 28, 1963, a young social worker (and later attorney) Fay Williams helped load men, women, and children onto buses at St. John's Missionary Baptist Church for the trip to the March on Washington for Jobs and Freedom. It was a scene being repeated at churches and community centers in towns across the United States. The trip to Washington, DC, from Indianapolis took about eight hours. People were excited, though they didn't know quite what to expect once they reached the nation's capital. "The atmosphere was celebratory not apprehensive," remembered Williams years later, even with the chance there could be violence. After all, said Williams, even President Kennedy did not think such a large gathering was a good idea.[6]

Buses from all over the country—yellow school buses and chartered city buses—pulled into Washington, and thousands of people, people as far as the eye could see, moved into the National Mall to march more than a mile from the Washington Monument to the Lincoln Memorial. Massed around the memorial's reflecting pool, they listened to music from Odetta, Mahalia Jackson, Joan Baez, and Bob Dylan. They listened to the day's sixth speaker, the young firebrand, head of the Student Nonviolent Coordinating Committee, and later Georgia congressman John Lewis, call for legislation "that will protect the Mississippi sharecropper who is put off his farm because he dares to register to vote."[7] And they listened to Martin Luther King Jr. deliver his "I Have a Dream" speech, the words of which would become iconic for the civil rights movement. The power—and peacefulness—surprised even the ten official sponsoring organizations. These included the Commission on Religion and Race, a new committee of Irwin Miller's organization, the National Council of Churches. In the report from the commission's young executive director, Dr. Robert Spike, there was a feeling of euphoria: "When the National Council of Churches delegation, over 100 strong, moved into the stream of marchers . . . one of the deepest longings of my ministry was for a moment fulfilled—the longing that the Church of Jesus Christ be in the *midst* of the human struggle, not on the sidelines."[8] Irwin Miller was not among the church leaders marching. Those who knew him suggest it was not his style to be in the limelight, out in front walking arm in arm with Martin Luther King Jr., Eugene Carson Blake, and other civil rights and religious leaders, black and white. But not being physically a part of the enormous outpouring of frustration and hope was one of his regrets, his oldest daughter Margaret would say many years later. In her opinion, his advisors at the National Council of Churches discouraged Miller from going, perhaps fearing he—and the organization—would appear too radical. Or perhaps there were concerns about possible violence. "He really regretted not going and taking us [his older children]."[9]

Less than one month later, on Sunday, September 15, came the bombing of the Sixteenth Street Baptist Church in Birmingham, Alabama, killing four little girls attending Sunday school. Three days later Irwin Miller, as chairman of President Kennedy's special committee on religion and race, was again in Washington, heading a meeting of twenty church leaders with key congressional leaders to call for swift passage of civil rights legislation. In a meeting with Attorney General Robert Kennedy, the group asked for more effective protection against racist "atrocities."[10] The delegation of church leaders from the Catholic, Protestant, and Jewish faiths urged their fellow clergy throughout the country to devote their upcoming sermons to the racial crisis. "Americans of every religious persuasion are yearning for a concrete way to express their moral outrage over the atrocities which had taken place," noted a press release from the National Council of Churches. "Our mourning will be empty unless out of this dark night of violence can come a new dawn of social and racial justice in our land."[11]

Before returning home from Washington, many of the religious leaders, though inexperienced at the Washington game of politics, stopped in the offices of their states' congressional delegations to urge support for upcoming civil rights legislation. "It is easy to see why the more experienced lobbyists of the Leadership Conference on Civil Rights from the labor unions and the National Association [for the Advancement] of Colored People (NAACP) welcomed them as full partners in the task of securing comprehensive civil rights legislation," wrote James F. Findlay Jr., author of *Church People in the Struggle*.[12]

As civil rights legislation made its way through Congress, Irwin Miller and his colleagues continued to apply pressure whenever they could. One of Miller's most effective tactics was to offer midwestern members of Congress a ride home aboard his private plane when he was leaving Washington. Once aloft, "he would lobby them relentlessly twenty-thousand feet in the air," wrote journalist and historian Clay Risen in his 2014 book *The Bill of the Century*. Minority Leader Everett Dirksen was considered a key player. Learning that Dirksen would be visiting his hometown of Pekin, Illinois, Miller and the Reverend Eugene Carson Blake traveled to central Illinois to lobby him personally. Dirksen eventually moved from opponent to "full-throated supporter."[13] One of the stalwarts leading opposition to such legislation was Georgia's Senator Richard Russell. He once complained to a friend, "We had been able to hold the line until all the churches joined the civil rights lobby in 1964."[14]

And then came Dallas.

With President Kennedy's assassination in November 1963, civil rights momentum passed on to the new president, Lyndon Baines Johnson, a southerner (well, a Texan), who picked up the sometimes sputtering torch. As presidential historian Doris Kearns Goodwin explained, "JFK set things in motion, LBJ carried through." But it took more than Kennedy, Johnson, and King. Author Clay Risen specifically lists "National Council of Churches president, J. Irwin Miller" among the black activists, labor leaders, religious leaders, and politicians who brought civil rights legislation to fruition. "The Civil Rights Act is often explained like a one-man play, when in fact it had a cast of thousands."[15]

After nine days of debate in the House of Representatives and a fifty-seven-day filibuster followed by eighty-three days of debate in the Senate, President Lyndon Johnson signed the Civil Rights Act on July 2, 1964. It declared that discrimination based on race, color, religion, sex, or national origin in voting, schools, public accommodations, and employment was illegal.[16]

Laws were crucial, but Irwin Miller had other areas through which he personally had the power to affect progress. Ten months before the Civil Rights Act was signed, in a September 19, 1963, memo, his office requested a one-page report from each of the family companies "advising the specific actions taken to promote racial equality recently and in the past . . . as evidence of each company's interest in promoting racial equality."[17] Irwin Union Bank reported both success and failures, mentioning "a young lady who is colored" who would be working as a secretary. (Well-intentioned white executives were having trouble finding the right words—colored? Negro? The terms *black* or *African American* were not yet common.) The bank also reported helping with the financing of a manse for Columbus's Second Baptist Church (a predominately black church).[18] Cummins's Atlas and Seymour crankshaft facilities reported thirty-six Negroes in the shop and five in the office.[19]

Cummins's personnel vice president reported "42 Negroes employed in various departments throughout the plant; some have been with us over 20 years. Employment standards are high; yet we have for many years drawn Negroes from the surrounding areas." Mentioned were a manager's secretary, two engineers, and one "Negro admitted to the Apprentice Program where standards are stringent. The Company aggressively is seeking qualified Negroes and members of other minority groups by determining the best sources of qualified personnel."[20] It would be some years later, according to Claudia Stevens Maddox, a systems analyst and Morgan State

University graduate who joined Cummins's IT department in 1988, that American corporations, including Cummins, would finally realize that among these best sources were the country's HBCUs—historically black colleges and universities—Howard, Morehouse, Morgan State, Spelman, and others.[21]

As for the city of Columbus, things were slow going. This was, after all, southern Indiana, a conservative part of a conservative state, though not necessarily more racist than other sections of the state. In the 1920s much of the state of Indiana had been fertile ground for Ku Klux Klan activity, though early Klan targets tended to be primarily Catholics, Jews, and "foreigners." Hoosiers could be narrow-minded, as well as proud and prickly. Indiana-born humorist and successful Broadway playwright George Ade once wrote about the state, "We have a full quota of smart alecks, but not one serf."[22] Though attitudes could be slow to change, Miller and his executives believed (perhaps hoped) that white Hoosiers could be convinced to accept a new way of thinking about whom they lived with, ate with, and worked with.

Cummins's executives asked Columbus lawyer Lee Hamilton, head of the mayor's civil rights committee (and soon to be Democratic congressman from Indiana's Ninth District) to draft a nondiscriminatory plank to be inserted in the platforms of a mayoral candidate and the Democratic Party. In a September 1963 memo, one Cummins executive reported, "I have requested that the Civil Rights Committee propose to the Mayor that he have a meeting, with some of them present, of all of the barbers, another of all of the restaurant operators, another the hotel and motel operators." This effort, he commented dryly, "has been non-productive as of this writing."[23] (Eventually some of the new Cummins employees hired a barber who knew how to cut black hair to drive down from Indianapolis a couple times a week.)[24]

Irwin Miller continued to push the town on its attitudes toward the diverse workforce he envisioned for Cummins. New black employees were still having trouble buying houses in some neighborhoods. This included James (Jim) A. Joseph, an ordained minister and civil rights activist and one of Miller's most important recruits. As associate director of the Cummins Engine Foundation, Jim Joseph brought his family to Columbus in the summer of 1967. "Even when I decided on a house, the neighbors got together and protested against my coming into the neighborhood," Joseph later remembered.

With demonstrations and riots erupting elsewhere in the country—Detroit and Newark, for instance—Miller addressed shareholders of the Irwin Bank. "We have examples on every side of communities who didn't solve their problems while they could, and now their cost will be staggering—civil disturbance dangerous in its proportions, and the possibility of imminent collapse. Will we have the foresight to learn from the experience of others? I think the next year or two will tell. And the real test will come in our own community response to discrimination, and specifically to the proposal for an open housing ordinance."[25] (Though slow, change did come. By the time she joined Cummins in 1988, Morgan State graduate Claudia Stevens Maddox, reported having no trouble finding the housing she wanted in Columbus.)[26]

After company clout helped the Joseph family buy a house, Joseph worked with the town's Human Relations Commission to develop the open-housing ordinance. When Joseph learned that the vote on the ordinance might come up short at the city council meeting, he asked Miller if he would address the meeting. Irwin Miller, Jim Joseph, and Philip Sorensen, head of the Cummins Engine Foundation, were among those attending the city council meeting on January 6, 1969, in support of a strong ordinance. Miller explained how Cummins had expanded into many countries and had worldwide sales. "We have a very active, I would say nervous concern that Columbus be a community where a person can live with equal rights with his neighbor."[27] His remarks, similar to his earlier letter to the mayor, contained a not-so-subtle warning: "No company can commit itself to further growth in a community that does not, in turn, commit itself to the elimination of discriminatory practices." At the city council meeting two weeks later, the open-housing ordinance passed by a vote of four to three.[28]

With encouragement from Joseph and with the issues of race and poverty added to its earlier focus on the town's physical environment (the architectural initiative), the Cummins Engine Foundation suggested a field officer project. Five black field officers would represent Cummins in the black communities of major US cities—Chicago, Washington, Los Angeles, Detroit, and Atlanta—with money to make community grants. Reports from the field officers "succeeded in steeping the white managers who ran Cummins in the realities of urban experience. This, it seems, was part of Irwin Miller's design from the start," said a later company history.[29] It was a two-way street—Cummins's white managers got educated and black communities got grants. Also, funds from the project "enhanced the capacity of the African-American communities to participate in leadership of those communities," explained Joseph.[30]

Jim Joseph left Columbus for a short period to serve as chaplain of Claremont Colleges in California. He came back in 1972 as a vice president reporting directly to president Henry Schacht. His duties included heading an informal overarching organization of the foundations through which the family and company funneled money into the community (and wider world): Cummins Engine Foundation, the family's Irwin-Sweeney-Miller Foundation, and the family bank's Irwin Union Foundation. He also became head of the Corporate Action Division, which intended to "serve as an in-house resource for understanding the social and political context in which the company does business." The division would "work with management at all levels to ensure that all business analyses—new plant sites, new ventures, market penetration, product development, functional planning, etc.—include corporate responsibility considerations."[31]

It was an ambitious agenda that kept Jim Joseph busy until he left Cummins for Washington, DC, in 1977 to serve as undersecretary of the Department of the Interior under President Jimmy Carter, the first of four American presidents under whom he would serve. In 1995 he was named US ambassador to South Africa. But his connections to Columbus would continue through the years as he served several terms on the Cummins Foundation Board. And it was Jim Joseph who passed along Martin Luther King Jr.'s compliment that put Irwin Miller's life and actions into a wider context. King, said Joseph, had once called Irwin Miller "the most socially responsible businessman in the country."[32]

Designer Alexander Girard's innovative conversation pit in Xenia and Irwin Miller's Eero Saarinen house enabled people sitting in the living room to enjoy Dan Kiley's landscape. *Carol Highsmith Collection, Library of Congress*

US Post Office,
side colonnade.
Kevin Roche. 1970.
Don Nissen, Columbus Visitors Center

11 Farewells

AT THE BEGINNING OF WHAT WOULD TURN OUT TO BE ONE OF America's most fractious decades, Irwin Miller was recruited to serve on the Yale Corporation Board, the organization that ran the university. From 1959 to 1977 Miller and approximately a dozen fellow trustees would spend one weekend a month during the academic year on the New Haven, Connecticut, campus that Miller had left thirty-some years earlier.[1] Anger over the Vietnam War, civil rights marches, and general frustration with what was termed "the Establishment" was particularly acute on college campuses. Miller was a fortuitous choice for these unsettled times. Not only was he one of the most financially generous board members (he and fellow board member John Hay "Jock" Whitney both gave more than $1 million during the 1960s), but he had strong beliefs that gave him the confidence to speak out. Miller "put backbone" into his corporation colleagues at board meetings around the large mahogany table in Woodbridge Hall.[2] Through his civil rights work in Washington with Kennedy and Johnson, Miller had been through some of this before. "In bringing his activism to his trusteeships, Miller motivated colleagues and institutions to seek progressive change," wrote

Geoffrey Kabaservice. He pushed them to modernize the institution, spurring them on "to make the controversial decisions that they knew were the correct ones."[3]

When alumni began to object to some of the board's decisions, Yale president Kingman Brewster asked Miller to answer their angry letters. Some, for instance, felt that honoring Martin Luther King Jr. was encouraging communism. "The menace and threat of worldwide Communism is a very real one," wrote Miller to one unhappy alum. "In my opinion we combat it best by making our country so strong and healthy, so clearly superior to competitive societies that the Communist virus finds no fertile soil among us. This means, among other things, the elimination of persistent poverty, the reduction of unemployment to levels well below those of other societies, and the extension of equal freedom, dignity, and opportunity to every segment of our people."[4] It was vintage Irwin Miller—gracefully written, reasonable, perceptive yet firm.

Miller, the experienced diesel engine man, had his own unique metaphor for moderate leaders like Brewster (and himself) "who tried to maintain the stability of their institutions and society while accommodating the engines of change." As Miller told author Geoffrey Kabaservice, "I'm an engine builder. If you build an engine without a governor, you never know when it's going to explode. But if it has a governor, it can do good work, and never to the point of destruction.[5]

Like many Republicans, by the mid-1960s Miller's attitude about the Vietnam War began to shift slowly. "I was a player a good deal of the time in the Johnson administration," he told Kabaservice. "Because of a couple of remarks from the president to me [I knew] Johnson never believed in the war, but he didn't know how in the hell to get out of it." Kabaservice explained that Miller "supported the Vietnam intervention until well into the 1960s, although with much squirming. The managerial outlook of men like Miller made it all but impossible for them to take issue publicly with friends' operations in their spheres of expertise." Miller recalled later, "I think anyone who's in a position of management is apt to be extremely reluctant to second guess somebody else. . . . He knows that choices are not usually between the good way and the bad way to do something but almost always between two bad ways."[6]

Yale president Kingman Brewster and Miller stayed friends even after Miller left the corporation board. Brewster left Yale to become US ambassador to Great Britain in 1977 and then master of University College, Oxford. When Brewster died in 1988, Miller spoke at his memorial service in Oxford.

> It is a sad fact that we humans all too often see a friend more clearly in death than in life. . . . He was the great American university president of his time and perhaps of this century. In a period of storm and upheaval and discontinuity he brought his institution through intact. He was always in charge, and he changed it in every important way for the better. He made it a model for his nation. We who knew him then now look back and see that he was among the very few who read his times correctly; that he intuitively made the right choices, and made them crisply. . . . Early in his tenure he single-handedly opened the undergraduate colleges to women. . . . He championed the cause of minorities in the whole of our society and received his bitterest criticism for so doing. . . . The attributes of both his leadership and his friendship that one remembers were in his own times rather out of fashion. You could gossip with him but you could not be petty. You could vent outrage, but you could not express hatred in his presence. You could laugh, but you could not ridicule. . . . We have lost a friend, and a man who in his life made a greater difference for good than most of us will be able to claim.[7]

In 1970 a green, young finance graduate from the University of Michigan was recruited by the Irwin Management Company as part of the philosophy of developing young talent. David Goodrich, like other newcomers, was invited to sit in the back of the room at Irwin

Miller's weekly meetings and observe. Miller, he saw, kept abreast of actions at Cummins and other family enterprises by asking questions. It was a technique that Miller had used ever since he had been dropped into top Cummins management in the 1930s as the totally inexperienced heir apparent. At these weekly meetings, Miller kept discussions on track. He kept an eye on the clock and the agenda. He was respectful but direct. He did not want a lot of explanation; he wanted answers. And if answers to his questions got too long and lost focus, he would politely interrupt, say thank you, and move on to his next question. He made it a point of honor that decisions not be postponed.

By now Irwin Miller's management style was well established. A fifteen-minute meeting meant fifteen minutes. He was known as a fierce competitor. He preached that a time of company success was a time of vulnerability. *We* should be our own biggest competitors, he often said, continually developing the next thing that will make our engines obsolete. He believed in putting competent young people in positions of great responsibility. Yes, they would make mistakes, but they would be risk-takers, would be forward-looking, and would think for themselves. But what always stayed with those who worked for and with Miller was his philosophy that the role of the business leader was more than financial, and more than just taking care of shareholders. The well-being of others—employees, customers, vendors, the community—was also important. The company benefited from balancing the interests of these five stakeholders. As some have pointed out, this was easier for Miller, since he and his family were major shareholders. In a way, he was answering to himself. Yet it was the emphasis on the fifth stakeholder—the community—that set Miller and the Cummins Engine Company apart.[8]

Over time, Clessie Cummins continued to distance himself financially from the company and geographically from Columbus. After serving as president and chairman, Cummins was gently being eased out, according to some observers.[9] In 1947, when the family's *preferred* stock went on the market, Cummins decided to place his *common* stock for sale. People who cared about Clessie tried to persuade him to hold on to his stock, "his only stake in the engine company."[10] The stock was expected to dramatically increase in value and dividends during the coming years. As explained in the thick company history *The Engine That Could,* commissioned by Cummins Engine Company and published by Harvard Business School Press in 1997, Clessie sold fifty thousand shares of common stock in 1947 (a significant part of his remaining shares) for about $1 million. If he had waited twenty years, those shares, added to the approximately twenty thousand he had already sold, would have been worth more than $33 million, plus $5 million just in dividends. "It seems clear that he sold the orchard just as the trees were beginning to bear," one observer later commented. "But Clessie had already waited twenty years for the orchard to bear," the Cummins history continued. "Financially and psychologically he could wait no longer."[11]

In July 1959 Cummins returned to Columbus for the ceremony marking the company's fortieth anniversary. Miller, who could not attend, had written a letter to be read at the occasion. He mentioned much that only he, Clessie, and a few others would remember from the company's early days:

- All the crises, where you saved the company from the buzz saw at the last minute,
- All the trips to W. G.'s office for $10,000 more,
- All the wonderful voyages on the river for "experimental" purposes,
- All the low-grade tricks on unsuspecting persons,
- All the razzle-dazzle publicity which made everyone think the company was ten times as important as it was,
- And all the genuine, fundamental thinking and real daring and courage which got the company off to an early, solid start, and laid the foundation on which others could build.
- For all these things we are grateful, and all of them we remember. Many happy returns on your Fortieth Anniversary.[12]

Forty-year pin? It was a bittersweet visit, Cummins's son Lyle would write in *The Diesel Odyssey of Clessie Cummins*. Cummins was hoping for an offer from the company for an improved hydraulic brake design he would receive a patent for in November 1965. But it was not to be.[13] The authors of *The Engine That Could* summarized it this way: "In retrospect, it was simply improbable that Clessie Cummins, working in his California garage in the late 1950s, could come up with the world's best engine brake. It was so improbable, in fact, that the brightest engineers at the Engine Company (and their counterparts at perhaps a half-dozen other companies) couldn't see Clessie's invention for what it was—'a wonderful product.' It was the last time, but far from the first time that Clessie's inventive genius was underestimated."[14]

By this time Cummins and his family had moved from Columbus to Northern California, living first in Hillside, then in a large, classic Monterey-style home in Palo Alto, and then at their one-thousand-acre working cattle ranch eighty miles south of San Francisco. Eventually they bought a house in Sausalito, high in the hills at the end of the Golden Gate Bridge across from San Francisco. Cummins turned his daylight basement into a machine shop for working on new inventions (several of his California inventions produced new patents), and it was only five minutes from where Cummins's most recent yacht was docked.[15] It was a nice life. Occasionally, Cummins's feelings of mistreatment by the Cummins Engine Company would erupt like hot lava, and historic disagreements would seep into the present. During other periods, however, the volcano would lie still under quiescent decades of friendship. The relationship would always be complicated.

During a peaceful period in 1960, Irwin and Xenia Miller were in San Francisco for a meeting of the National Council of Churches, at which Irwin Miller became the first layman elected president of the organization. The Millers invited Clessie and Stella Cummins to the installation celebration. The four were standing together after the ceremony when California governor Pat Brown walked by. Miller expressed a desire to meet him, and Cummins brought him over and introduced him. After they had an opportunity to chat and the governor had left, Miller asked Cummins how he happened to know the governor. "Know him? I've never seen him before," said Cummins, with great enjoyment at Miller's astonishment.[16]

In August 1968 Cummins died in his sleep at his home in Sausalito at the age of seventy-nine. An inventor to the end, he had been working earlier in the evening in his home shop on a prototype of a new engine. At a meeting of the Cummins board of directors six weeks later, a special resolution was adopted that read in part: "Clessie Lyle Cummins founded this Company as a young man possessed of neither money nor formal education, only determination and authentic genius. In the tradition of the great American inventors, his designs more often than not appeared before their time, and a later generation and another technology were required to demonstrate their full worth."[17] The remarks Irwin Miller delivered at the memorial service in Columbus were more personal:

> Clessie Cummins was my best friend. He taught me how to shoot a gun. He taught me how to navigate the Ohio River after dark. And he taught me about business.
>
> We began all this before I was ten years old. Although there was twenty years' difference in our ages, I cannot remember a time when we did not deal with each other as contemporaries. We had furious arguments—over guns, boats, business, whether a car got better gas mileage in level or hilly country, and whether the New Deal was wholly evil or was there some small word of good to be said about it. In all these arguments we carefully avoided reference to the facts, because they might have settled the argument, and that would have been somehow like the death of an old friend.
>
> I always understood that if I were ever to be in real trouble, Clessie was not only willing to stand by and help, but was also the kind of person who would go down with you if you went down.[18]

These were affectionate, warm words, but words by Irwin Miller many years later would probably have pleased Cummins just as much, or maybe more. "We made a big mistake in not buying and producing Clessie's brake," Miller told the authors of *The Engine That Could*. "There was a certain amount of 'not invented here' in our engineering department. 'We can do a better brake than that in six months,' they were saying, 'so we don't have to buy that.' Ten years went by and we never developed our own."[19]

Chicago's Harry Weese, right, not only designed more buildings in Columbus than any other architect but also did work in the Miller family compound in Muskoka, Canada. *Irwin-Sweeney-Miller Collection, Indiana Historical Society*

Cummins chairman Irwin Miller (*center*) was on hand in September 1964 when the company was listed on the New York Stock Exchange under the symbol CUM. *Cummins Inc., Irwin-Sweeney-Miller Collection, Indiana Historical Society*

Muskoka, in northern Ontario, was the location for many family vacations. *Left to right, back row*: Bob Tangeman, Betsey, Clementine, Irwin, and Margaret; *front row*: Elsie, Hugh, Xenia, Will, Genevieve the dog, and Catherine. *Irwin-Sweeney-Miller Collection, Indiana Historical Society*

Large Arch.
Henry Moore. 1971.
Carol M. Highsmith,
Library of Congress

12 The Kiss

IT HAD BEEN A LONG JOURNEY. FROM A SCULPTOR'S STUDIO IN THE English countryside, to a foundry in Germany, across the ocean to the port of New Orleans, on a barge up the Mississippi and Ohio Rivers, and finally up an interstate (a snug fit on bridges) through southern Indiana to a large open square in front of the new Bartholomew County Library in Columbus, Indiana. It had been the idea of I. M. Pei, the library's architect, to have a massive bronze piece commissioned from his friend, the esteemed English sculptor Henry Moore. *Large Arch,* as it was titled, would supply the massive bulk required to anchor the plaza, surrounded as it was by the library, the Irwin house and gardens to the east, and Eliel Saarinen's First Christian Church across the street. There had been two important stipulations. The opening had to be large enough for people to stroll through, requested Pei. Moore agreed but did not want it to be large enough for a car to drive through. "'As a young sculptor I saw Stonehenge and ever since I've wanted to do work that could be walked through and around,' Moore had explained."[1]

The abstract, towering sculpture was indeed large—nineteen and a half feet high by twelve and a half feet at its base. It weighed five and a half tons. The previous summer, Xenia and Irwin Miller, who were making a gift of the sculpture to the town, had driven up from London to visit Moore and his wife at their home and studio in Hertfordshire. At the time the plaster model was off in Berlin being sand-cast in bronze in fifty segments. "Quite a big undertaking," Moore had informed Miller—and that was an understatement.[2] By April 1971 the sculpture, its surface "patinated" a muted green by the artist before it left Berlin, was in place on the library plaza. The segments had been welded together with nearly invisible seams. Classes at two nearby schools had been dismissed so that several hundred children could watch the arch being put in place. Miller reported to Moore that his reaction was "beyond description." He wrote, "It is not my habit to speak extravagantly [another understatement], so you must know that I write out of a very deep response to this noble work. . . . The community comes to see it, touch it, walk round and through it, sketch it until late hours at night."[3]

Another member of the community, Ninth District congressman Lee Hamilton, who had helped with the many permits and arrangements necessary to ship the arch to its new home, sent Miller his reaction a few weeks later. "Initially, I was puzzled," wrote Hamilton, "and the question on my mind was 'What is it?' and 'What was the artist trying to communicate?'. . . I walked around it, viewed it more carefully and found it held a peculiar attraction. It conveyed an elemental force, a strength that appealed to me. . . . You might also like to know the enthusiastic reaction I encountered from a teenage girl when I asked her how she liked it. Her response was, 'Oh, it's marvelous. My boyfriend and I were the first ones to kiss under the arch.'" Hamilton continued, "You just may have started a tradition that even Henry Moore did not anticipate."[4] *Large Arch* may never remind anyone of Auguste Rodin's *The Kiss*, but apparently both celebrated the same romantic human impulse. Moore's work was generally extremely popular in the United States. At the time of his death, art critic John Russell, writing in the *New York Times*, would mention his four major public sculptures in Princeton, New Jersey, Chicago, New York, and Columbus, Indiana.[5]

Congressman Lee Hamilton was again helpful when it came time to build a new US post office in downtown Columbus. The postal department was accustomed to using its own traditional designs produced by its own staff of designers. Columbus, however, now an acclaimed architectural boomtown, had its own ideas. Hamilton had a good relationship with Larry O'Brien, the postmaster general. On one of Cummins executive Dick Stoner's trips to Washington, O'Brien and Hamilton took Stoner to the Oval Office to see the president. At the end of their conversation, President Johnson (LBJ) turned to O'Brien and said, "Larry, you give Hamilton anything he wants."[6] Kevin Roche's post office, with architectural design fees paid by the Cummins Foundation, was dedicated in July 1970. Constructed of sand-glazed dark, reddish-brown tiles, it had a dramatic colonnade along one side formed by massive, square columns. It was the first US post office designed by a privately funded architect.[7]

❧ ❧ ❧

The Millers continued their friendship with the occupants of the White House. After Lady Bird's stop in Columbus on her Midwest beautification tour, Xenia and Irwin Miller were invited to a state dinner for the prime minister of Japan in November 1967 and an overnight stay at the White House, along with several other couples. Mid-November was the end of an Indian summer, Mrs. Johnson noted in her informal White House social diary. "The golden leaves of the ginkgo trees had fallen like a dropped cloak around the trunks."[8]

When arranging seating at the tables for the two hundred guests attending the formal banquet, Mrs. Johnson made certain to place Irwin Miller between "two of the brightest women I know" (Elspeth and Libby Rowe) and close to CBS president Frank Stanton.[9] After dinner and a dessert called strawberry Yamaguchi and entertainment by singer Tony Bennett, Lady Bird led the five couples who were overnight guests upstairs for a nightcap—"something I always look forward to," she noted. They talked about the recent article in *Life* magazine about Miller and Columbus architecture.[10] Miller reported on his recent visit with Mayor John Lindsay of New York and his tour of Bedford-Stuyvesant. "The gist of it [Miller's report] was this is the first civilization where there has been enormous affluence and at the same time a degrading poverty that is side by side and invisible," Lady Bird summarized in her diary. "I like exploring ideas," she continued. "I have the feeling that this man [Miller] found it time wasted fully with just chattering small talk."

President Johnson, in his pajamas, came in briefly to greet the group and then headed off to bed—"Quite weary," noted his wife. Just a month earlier an estimated one hundred thousand Vietnam War protestors had gathered at the Lincoln Memorial.[11] Questions about Vietnam and whether LBJ would run again for president were working their way through official and unofficial Washington. But despite national tensions, the Millers were still able to enjoy their "memorable night in the White House,"[12] as Xenia Miller called it in her thank-you note to the First Lady. Irwin Miller sent a separate note. "It is a very great achievement, in the midst of the extraordinary responsibilities which each of you bear, to maintain an atmosphere of such gracious concern for others," he wrote. "Our prayers are with you and your husband in these most difficult of times."[13]

Back in Indiana Irwin Miller had several pieces of interesting advice for the young talent moving to Columbus and joining the Cummins organization. He told one group of new hires to be wary of the company taking over their entire lives: the company would take all of their time if they let it.[14] He told Henry Schacht, Jim Henderson, and John Hackett, who would eventually take top positions at

Cummins, that he had learned the hard way that it was sometimes difficult to get a variety of opinions in a small town in Indiana. He recommended, therefore, that they expand their horizons by joining the boards of directors of two business corporations and of at least one nonprofit.

Miller had followed his own advice. Some of the organizations to which Miller gave time as a trustee included the Ford Foundation, the Museum of Modern Art in New York, the Mayo Foundation, AT&T, Equitable Life Insurance Society, the National Humanities Center, and Chemical Bank.[15] Closer to home he served on the boards of Butler University (with connections to the family through his father, mother, and great-uncle) and Christian Theological Seminary (CTS), both in Indianapolis.

Through the years he served on many national governmental and presidential commissions, before and after his civil rights work for Presidents Kennedy and Johnson. These included the Commission of Money and Credit; Special Committee on US Trade with East European Countries and the Soviet Union, as chairman; National Advisory Commission on Health Manpower, as chairman; President's Committee on Urban Housing; President's Commission on Postal Organization; Study Commission on US Policy toward Southern Africa; and, internationally, on the United Nations' Commission on Multinational Corporations. It was a daunting list, but Miller, always a quick study, stayed on top of things with a devoted and efficient office staff in Columbus and a company plane at the ready. His staff prepared their boss by digesting the reams of reports that flowed into Columbus before board meetings and then presenting Miller with summaries. The board positions may have required varying amounts of hands-on effort from Miller, yet all required time away from Columbus.

Though there was nearly unanimous respect for Miller's opinions and advice, "he was not a naturally gifted orator," said Congressman Lee Hamilton. "He had no inflection in his voice. He read everything."[16] At a hearing before a Senate committee about foundations and taxes, Miller, who was at that point a Ford Foundation trustee and, of course, had his own family foundation, was chosen to be the lead-off witness in the discussion of the role of foundations in American life. "He did not handle it very well," remembered one member of the testifying group. "He didn't bring out the points very clearly and we were all very distressed at that. . . . I was surprised at how nervous he was, for a man of his great experience and reputation." Miller was "not really as outspoken as his written testimony," said another.[17]

Written communications were another matter. When he was in Congress, Lee Hamilton would hear frequently from Miller. "He wrote the finest letters to politicians I ever read—one page, one topic, remarks right on the mark. He was courteous and thought very carefully about an issue. He kept close contact on what I did."

Through the years Xenia Miller had risen to the challenge of upholding the family tradition of noblesse oblige by serving on many arts and community boards. With aplomb she entertained Rockefellers, First Ladies, and other national figures, such as poet W. H. Auden, who spoke at the dedication of the I. M. Pei library. She was a trustee of Christian Theological Seminary and was credited with choosing or commissioning much of the art that graced the long halls of Edward Larabee Barnes's glass-walled building. She received an honorary degree from CTS in 1998.[18] She was also a trustee at large of the Indianapolis Museum of Art. For many years she would lend her ceramic hill town to the museum during the holiday season. "Italian Village (Citta di Casteltauro)," was the work of Giancarlo Girard, Alexander Girard's brother. More than five feet high (including the base on which it was placed), it towered over the museum's younger visitors who searched each year for the tiny ceramic cat sunning on the roof of one of the tiny ceramic houses. Xenia Miller had developed her own discriminating eye as a collector, particularly of folk art. When she and Irwin Miller traveled, she often visited art museums or galleries, and he often attended a symphony or other musical performance.[19]

Aunt Elsie Sweeney also did much entertaining at Castalia, her dazzlingly unusual house on Harrison Lake west of Columbus. Built in 1963 and designed to Sweeney's specifications by Indianapolis architect Tom Dorste, the twenty-room house had terrazzo floors, an inner courtyard with fountain, and four sides of high, gleaming white arches. There Sweeney, a classically trained pianist, would host musical soirees and other fund-raisers, featuring guest artists such as André Watts and Van Cliburn. Some reported seeing white swans swimming in the lake. Architecturally Castalia was a far cry from the lean, simple modernist buildings her nephew favored. And perhaps that was the point.[20]

In early 1977 Irwin Miller stepped down as chairman of the Cummins board of directors, a position he had held since 1951. He was leaving the day-to-day running of the company in experienced hands. Henry Schacht, president since 1969, would be the new chairman of the board. Jim Henderson would replace Schacht as Cummins president and continue as chief operating officer. Miller, as chairman of the executive and finance committees, would stay involved, picking the brains of people he would invite for lunch at his office at 301 Washington Street and sending pithy, sometimes wryly humorous memos to Cummins staff members.

A few years later, beginning in late 1988, the Miller family—Irwin, Xenia, and Clementine—would become involved in the affairs of Cummins in a major way. When a British industrial conglomerate, Hanson PLC, was divulged as the buyer of a significant amount of Cummins stock (8.3 percent), the company, the town, and Wall Street wondered about Hanson's intentions. Was Hanson an investor in Cummins, or was an unfriendly takeover on the horizon? Thirty-two-year-old Will Miller, with a graduate business degree from Stanford after following in his father's footsteps to Taft and Yale, was credited with coming up with the solution. He was now head of Irwin Management Company, which handled the family's investments and philanthropic activities. As a representative of the family, he had joined Henry Schacht in a mad scramble to find potential saviors/investors. Nothing had worked.

If Hanson took over Cummins and acted as it had in other takeovers, there would be inevitable losses to the town of Columbus. Irwin Management Company would have to make significant philanthropic expenditures to backstop those losses, Will Miller pointed out. What if the family instead did "preventive philanthropy," getting out ahead of the consequences of an unfriendly takeover? Irwin, Xenia, and Clementine (who held more stock than any other individual) agreed. The family would re-leverage its holdings and pay a premium above the stock's actual market price—in other words, greenmail. The Miller family paid 7.2 percent *above* the actual stock price for Hanson's one million or so shares of Cummins. Hanson made a $17 million return on its original investment, and the town's largest employer remained in Columbus.[21]

FIRE STATION
4

Fire Station No. 4.
Robert Venturi. 1968.
Carol M. Highsmith, Library of Congress

13 Mandela

THE ORNATE, GOLD-TIPPED GATES TO NEW YORK'S METROPOLITAN Club, the historic lair of Morgans and Vanderbilts on East Sixtieth Street just off Central Park, had seldom welcomed such an interesting and varied group. Arriving for a board meeting and luncheon were former government leaders of both parties, male and female corporate CEOs, a Cherokee Indian chief (female), and the tall, smiling man of the hour, South Africa's Nelson Mandela. Mandela was in New York to make a personal pitch to the members of the newly formed South Africa Free Elections Fund (SAFE). The organization might help to determine South Africa's future course, attendees had been told. Would the country's first post-apartheid elections produce a new democracy, or would the country descend into chaos?

Irwin Miller had flown in on the Cummins company plane early on the day of the luncheon, September 18, 1993. "Very important," Miller had noted on the invitation that had arrived only a week earlier. Miller, now in his mid-eighties, was increasingly likely to pass on meetings he did not consider important. "I apologize for the shortness of this notice, but Dr. Mandela's visit was unexpected and is likely to be his last before the April 1994 elections," wrote SAFE chairman Tony O'Reilly, the Irish-born former professional rugby player who was now chairman, president, and CEO of H. J. Heinz Company.

Miller had been recruited for the SAFE board by Wayne Fredericks, a fellow Indiana native who had been a deputy assistant secretary of state for African affairs in the 1960s. He had known Miller at the Ford Foundation, where Miller served on the foundation's Study Commission on US Policy toward Southern Africa. "A formidable task looms," Fredericks wrote in his letter to Miller. "Some 80% of the eligible electorate, the black population, has never voted." SAFE would raise funds from American corporations and foundations to fund the education of these new voters and would cease to exist after the elections, Fredericks assured Miller.[1] Mandela had originally called for twenty corporations to each donate $250,000 (or 1 million rand) toward a goal of $10 million. In his speech to the SAFE board members gathered at the Metropolitan Club, Mandela used a bit of humor. "I say in the United States you have the wealth of the whole universe concentrated here. I don't want checks from you; I want your checkbooks."[2]

When he returned from New York, Miller sent a memo to Cummins president Henry Schacht. "Ford has pledged $250,000. Frank Thomas [president of the Ford Foundation and a Cummins board member] suggested $50,000 for CEF [Cummins Engine Foundation]. The matter is now in your hands. Parenthetically, had interesting conversation with Mandela," continued the memo. "Will tell you about it."[3] Miller and his sister Clementine contributed an additional $1,500 from the family foundation.

The apartheid government had earlier asked Cummins, which had a twenty percent share of the South African diesel engine market in the late 1970s, to build new manufacturing facilities there. Miller and the Cummins board had sent a positive response, if (a large *if* as it turned out) Cummins was allowed to do business as it always had—with an integrated workforce and with no restrictions on hiring at any level, including supervisors. South African officials declined. Cummins forfeited all of its South African business. The board needed less than five minutes to make the decision, reported Cummins president Schacht with pride. (The German firm Daimler-Benz took over the South African diesel business when Cummins pulled out, and that "interesting conversation" Miller had had with Mandela may have been Mandela discussing Cummins's return to his country.)[4]

Miller was invited to Pretoria for Mandela's inauguration in May 1994. "This will be one of the great moments of this century," responded Miller, who nevertheless declined the invitation. "Unfortunately there is no way I can change my affairs to permit my being present," he wrote.[5] The Millers had previously visited Cummins dealers in South Africa, and their credentials with the new regime were good. But Irwin and Xenia Miller were now both in their eighties, and long, demanding trips, even in a private company plane, were less frequent.

One of the important items on Miller's calendar that was perhaps keeping him at home occurred in Columbus in June 1994—a two-day convening of the prestigious international Pritzker Architecture Prize. This prize (that some call a Nobel Prize for architecture) was being awarded in 1994 to a fifty-year-old French architect, Christian de Portzamparc. The eight-person jury (including such well-known American names as Frank Gehry and Ada Louise Huxtable) cited his architecture as being "bound by neither classicism nor modernism." It was "characterized by seeing buildings, their functions and the life within them, in new ways that require wide-ranging, but thoughtful exploration for unprecedented solutions."[6] Even if Portzamparc's roofs that soared, swooped, and hovered (in Huxtable's phrase) were not ever likely to land on elementary school buildings in southern Indiana, seeing "buildings, their functions and the life within them in new ways" was something Columbus could relate to. Interestingly, four of the former winners of the prize, Kevin Roche,

I. M. Pei, Richard Meier, and Robert Venturi, were represented by buildings in Columbus. Architects, critics, and the international panel of jurors toured the town to see firsthand (and more importantly on-site) its amazing architectural gems. A panel at the I. M. Pei library discussed "What Good Architecture Means to a Small Town."

Later the official laureate presentation was made at a banquet in César Pelli's glass-walled Commons, with Pelli on hand and the mechanical wheels and struts of Jean Tinguely's sculpture *Chaos I* hanging overhead. France was represented by its minister of culture, who spoke of his pleasure of seeing the wonderful collection of art and architecture "under the sun of Indiana."[7] During the conference, speakers quoted the late art historian Lord Kenneth Clark, a former Pritzker juror, who said that the Pritzker Prize would focus public attention on architecture, "a branch of human endeavor by which our civilization will be judged in the future." Lord Clark had continued, "A great historical episode can exist in our imagination almost entirely in the form of architecture. Very few of us have read the texts of early Egyptian literature. Yet we feel we know those infinitely remote people almost as well as our immediate ancestors chiefly because of their sculpture and architecture."[8] Speakers praised Irwin Miller, though he had insisted ahead of time that his name not be mentioned. "You can see how well we have lived up to that already tonight," said one speaker, who added that before he arrived in Columbus, he never before had a cab driver who "knew the difference between I. M. Pei and Robert Venturi."[9]

One of the more intimate events during the celebration was a dinner hosted by Xenia and Irwin Miller at their home. The honored guest was Jay Pritzker, the cofounder of the Hyatt Hotels chain, who had begun the annual architectural award in 1979. Also attending were such luminaries as the French minister of culture and Pritzker jurors and previous winners, including architect Kevin Roche, who, as Eero Saarinen's young principal design associate, had helped design the house in which the dinner was being held. (Roche's other Columbus buildings, in addition to the post office, included North Christian Church with Saarinen, Cummins's Walesboro plant, the visionary Cummins Corporate Office Building with verdant, trellised side garden, and renovations or additions to four other Columbus buildings.)

After the elaborate dinner at the Millers' home (including thirty soufflés, none of which fell), the group moved into the living room, and Miller brought out his Stradivarius. Joined by a small orchestra of faculty musicians from the school of music at nearby Indiana University, Miller and friends played Bach—superbly. Eighteenth-century German counterpoint filled the balmy summer night, leaving the guests wide-eyed. This was not Greenwich, Connecticut, or Houston's River Oaks, or any of the country's other affluent centers of sophistication. This was rural southern Indiana. When the evening was over, Pritzker said to Miller, "You really know how to make a guy feel small."[10] Many years later, architect Kevin Roche would remark, "I have always cherished that memory."[11]

Columbus City Hall. Edward Charles Bassett, Skidmore, Owings & Merrill. 1981. *Carol M. Highsmith, Library of Congress*

14 Bach

IF THERE WAS ONE WAY IN WHICH PEOPLE DID NOT GENERALLY understand Irwin Miller, it was in thinking that architecture was his prime interest among the arts. He liked and appreciated architecture, and it had served his purposes for Cummins and Columbus. But his passion was music.[1] His Stradivarius went to the Taft School with him and even through the north woods to Muskoka. It went with him to Yale Corporation meetings, where he and William Sloane Coffin on occasion played piano/violin duets.[2] His children remembered drifting off to sleep at night to the sound of their father playing Beethoven or Bach. Bach would be an important presence at Miller's funeral and memorial services, which he had begun planning. "The one thing I am adamant on is that my memorial service should include the music of J. S. Bach."[3]

Years earlier Clementine Tangeman, while living in New York, had made it possible for the young professional violinist Cho-Liang (Jimmy) Lin to use her Strad as he launched his career. Lin planned a concert in Columbus as a thank-you. It was on this occasion that Jimmy Lin first met Irwin Miller. Though the concert would be held in North Christian Church, many hours of rehearsing took place in the Millers' living room. Irwin Miller sat in the sunken conversation pit listening, simply listening, Lin remembered. And then he got out his double violin case and showed Lin his Stradivarius and Guarneri Del Gesu.[4]

Despite his service on many boards, Miller made time for violin practice. He studied seriously with violin maestro Josef Gingold, making the hour drive to Bloomington where Gingold was on the faculty at Indiana University. Gingold was once asked how good Miller was as a violinist. Gingold replied that he would make a very good concert master at a medium-sized symphony orchestra.[5] Gingold, a beloved teacher, was a prodigy born in Belorussia who had played with several renowned American orchestras. He suggested that his adopted midwestern home state launch an international violin competition, to be known as the International Violin Competition of Indianapolis, that would bring the world's best young violinists to Indianapolis every four years.

Irwin Miller was asked to be chairman of the advisory board for the first competition. Tom Beczkiewicz, founding director of the competition, assumed he was getting a high-profile board chairman who would be a figurehead. He soon learned differently. "When he [Miller] gets involved, he is involved," remembered Beczkiewicz. "What are you doing about medals for the winners?" Miller asked at one of their planning luncheons in his Washington Street office. "Bronze, silver, and gold vermeil," said Beczkiewicz. "No, vermeil is not gold," replied Miller. The first-place medal was switched to the real thing. He also asked to see the preliminary sketches for the medals' bas-relief sculpture of a hand holding a violin. The position of the hand on the violin was slightly wrong, pointed out Miller. It was corrected. Beczkiewicz explained that Miller taught him to go for the best, and that affected all the decisions Beczkiewicz subsequently made for the competition[6]. Emphasis on quality paid off, and in future years the musical world would rattle off the names

"Tchaikovsky, Queen Elisabeth, Indianapolis" when talking about the world's leading competitions for young musicians.

Inevitably, Xenia and Irwin Miller slowed down in their later years. In the Columbus house, an attractive but sturdy handrail had been installed by the steps leading down into the conversation pit. Their more extensive travels had been curtailed, but they still traveled to Hobe Sound, Florida, their winter home on Jupiter Island. There Miller began writing his memories in a green composition book, possibly as the basis for a future memoir. When organist, pianist, and future head of the Indiana University Music School Charles Webb and his wife would visit, there would be duets—the Handel G minor Sonata, perhaps, or other pieces in the piano/violin repertoire. "He knew what he could do and couldn't do," remembered Webb. "He would not attempt Mendelssohn or Tchaikovsky, but he could handle Handel."[7]

"Irwin was absolutely secure in his playing," said violinist Jimmy Lin, a Hobe Sound houseguest when he was in Florida for a concert in West Palm Beach. Every two years or so, Lin had been checking with Miller to see if he was interested in selling his 1715 Stradivarius, known as the Titian Strad. His answer had always been not yet. But Miller did not forget. After his death, a clause in his will instructed that Lin be contacted first when the estate was ready to sell the valuable instrument.[8]

As more years passed, Irwin and Xenia Miller were no longer able to get out into the world. Now the world came to them. Elders from North Christian Church brought communion to the Millers at their home. Among other visitors was former Cummins chairman Henry Schacht. He and Miller sat at a small table in the corner of the Millers' large living room and talked about things that had happened and the things that were, inevitably, about to happen. The talk turned to religion. One of Miller's comments was particularly significant. "I am looking forward to finding out if what I believed my whole life is true or not," said Miller, still cheerfully willing to accept the possibility of doubt within his lifelong religious beliefs.[9]

In May 2004 the Miller children and grandchildren arrived in Columbus for the celebration of Irwin's ninety-fifth birthday. In July there was one last trip to Muskoka. For this trip the Cummins Hawker 802 CE, with Will Miller on board, left Columbus and flew up to Rochester, Minnesota, to pick up Irwin Miller, who was at the Mayo Clinic to see if anything more could be done for his congestive heart failure. After being told the answer was no, the plane headed northeast to the small airport at Muskoka.[10]

Some years earlier, Llanrwst, the Eero Saarinen house on Lake Rosseau, had been partially damaged by lightning. When it had been rebuilt, changes had been made to accommodate the wheelchair that Miller now used much of the time. The rest of the family was there, and Miller showed interest in the studies and career plans of his grandchildren. He seemed more engaged than he had been in some time.[11] But even the magic of Muskoka could not halt the inexorable passage of time. Three days after returning to Columbus, Irwin Miller died at his home on Monday, August 16, 2004. He was ninety-five.

Private family graveside services took place the following Friday, and an afternoon memorial service was held the next day at Eero Saarinen's North Christian Church. As Miller had instructed, the service was similar to services for Clementine Tangeman, who had died in 1996, and for Aunt Elsie Sweeney, who had died in 1972.[12] More than five hundred people, many from out of town, filled the church. They were there to celebrate the remarkable life of their departed colleague, boss, neighbor, friend, father, and grandfather. The organ played Brahms, Teschner, Purcell, and of course Bach, including "Before Thy Throne I Stand," said to be a chorale prelude that Bach had selected for his own funeral.[13] Georg Neumark's 1641 hymn was the service's final hymn. "If thou but suffer God to guide thee, and hope in Him through all the ways," sang the congregation.

"He'll give thee strength, whate'er betides thee, and bear thee through the evil days; who trusts in God's unchanging love, Builds on the rock that naught can move."[14] The G-minor chords and words of the German hymn, plaintive but at the same time hopeful, soared aloft in the hexagonal, light-filled sanctuary.

Three weeks later in a letter to the Miller family from "our own little corner of Muskoka," the modest Windermere United Church remembered its "highly regarded neighbor," J. Irwin Miller. "Our thoughts and prayers are with those entrusted to honor his memory in a world so badly in need of role models like him. May his kindness and faith serve as a beacon to others."[15]

FACING, After performing a concert in Columbus, violinist Cho-Liang (Jimmy) Lin poses with Irwin and Clementine and their instruments, though for fun Irwin is holding Clementine's 1734 Guarneri del Gesu and Clementine holds her brother's 1715 Titian Stradivarius. Jimmy Lin acquired the famous Titian after Miller's death. It was so named because of its reddish-orange hue. *Jimmy Lin photo*

ABOVE, Irwin Miller greets President Lyndon Johnson at the White House. As president of the National Council of Churches, Miller worked on civil rights legislation with Johnson and his predecessor, President John Kennedy, leading up to the passage of the historic 1964 Civil Rights Act. *Cummins Inc., Irwin-Sweeney-Miller Collection, Indiana Historical Society*

Hamilton Center Ice Arena.
Harry Weese. 1958.
Don Nissen,
Columbus Visitors Center

15 AKA Pop

EIGHT YEARS BEFORE HIS DEATH—BUT PERHAPS GLIMPSING THE finish line in the distance—Irwin Miller wrote a letter to his five children. In it he tried to impress upon them the responsibilities that would be theirs with the sizeable amount of money they would inherit. "Of all the things we can 'leave to you,' money seems to us to be the least important. . . . We have not lived and worked primarily to maximize your inheritance any more than our ancestors lived and worked to maximize our inheritance. . . . We have worked and lived to make a constructive contribution to our community, church, and nation. And—we have had a good time so doing." The letter was signed J. I. M. (aka Pop).[1]

But just as the farmer has no control over what eventually happens to the wheat he plants and tends, Irwin and Xenia Miller, like many others who oversaw family fortunes, had no control over family actions and relationships after they were no longer on the scene, other than the plentiful examples from their own lives. Xenia Miller died in February 2008 at age ninety after years of being wrapped in a fog of severe dementia and four years after her husband's death. Luckily neither lived to see the family turmoil in the following years, though most of the relationships eventually healed.

Hugh Miller, fourth of the Millers' five children and five years older than Will, had been on the outs with the rest of the family for many years. Now living in Michigan, he brought suit against the estate's two trustees, his brother Will and Sarla Kalsi, longtime family financial advisor and CEO of Irwin Management Company. Hugh Miller's complaints concerned their management of Xenia Miller in her final days and the use of estate funds for maintenance of the family homes in Columbus and Muskoka. Will Miller had bought the big brick Irwin-Sweeney-Miller family house and gardens at 608 Fifth Street from the estate (at the request of his parents so that it could be used as a family guest house). Hugh Miller particularly objected to estate funds being used for its upkeep. Even earlier, while his father was still alive, Hugh Miller had suggested that Muskoka be carved up and he and his family be given a portion to avoid "problems of other families in similar situations." Instead, Irwin urged his children to cooperate in their management of Muskoka. "We have all this time treated it [Muskoka] as a 'spiritual' investment. We have never divided it up."[2]

As the legal proceedings moved forward at an almost Dickensian, Jarndyce-and-Jarndyce pace (as portrayed in Dickens's novel *Bleak House*), lawyers and others with business in the Bartholomew County Courthouse in downtown Columbus frequently dropped by the second-floor Superior Court Room 1 to see the drama of brother suing brother. Wrote one of the Indianapolis attorneys representing Will Miller: "What really brings this matter to court appears to be the psyche of Hugh Miller." Hugh, the attorney wrote, "has transferred his resentment over his poor relationship with his father into harboring an ill will towards his younger brother, with whom his parents had a much better and more trusting relationship." Said Hugh's attorney, "It is a matter of principle. He [Hugh] felt that someone had to stand up for his mother," (who had been incapacitated by dementia).[3] A law professor told a reporter for the *Indianapolis Business Journal* that money is never the real issue in fights surrounding inheritance and estates. "They're about the family dynamics. It's easier to blow up after somebody's gone."[4] And Irwin and Xenia Miller were both now gone. In November 2009, after two years of hearings, a Bartholomew County judge issued a ruling in favor of Will Miller and Kalsi.[5] So did the Indiana Appellate Court judge nine months later.

For Will Miller the conflicts over his parents' estate were part of an almost biblical, Job-like load. The family's 138-year-old Irwin Union Bank and Trust Company, which he headed, had collapsed after the housing market crash of 2008. Under Will's leadership, the bank, part of Irwin Financial Corporation, had invested aggressively—some in town said too aggressively—in subprime mortgages, particularly in growth states such as California and Nevada. But Will Miller had worked out a solution, said Henry Schacht, Miller's friend and former Cummins CEO. "This [the bank's closing] didn't have to happen, should not have happened." The US Treasury Department accepted Miller's plan, but the Chicago Federal Reserve did not.[6] "We were too heavily involved across the board in real estate," admits David Goodrich, a bank director. "When the market tanked in 2008–2009, anyone who was heavily involved in real estate got hurt. I thought, as the other directors did, or we wouldn't have gone along with it, that the business strategy as outlined by management made sense. But when everything caved in at once, we got caught up in it. And the Federal Reserve had bigger fish to fry. I will tell you what J. P. Morgan Chase did was much more egregious than anything we ever did. They were too big to fail, but we weren't. They saved the big guys." All involved with the bank "were wounded" by the outcome, said Goodrich, particularly Miller. "He did not deserve what happened."[7]

In September 2009 the bank notified the Federal Deposit Insurance Corporation that it was unable to raise the required capital to become solvent. On September 18, bank regulators announced publicly that Irwin Union Bank and Trust Company, the bank that had started with a safe in Joseph Irwin's Columbus dry goods store back in the 1860s, was sold to First Financial Bank of Cincinnati.[8]

But Columbus and those who cared about the Miller family legacy were ready for a little balance. The opportunity came in August 2009, the year of what would have been J. Irwin Miller's one hundredth birthday. It was also the fifth anniversary of his death. The setting was in the Red Room, the large red-carpeted community meeting room on the lower level of I. M. Pei's Bartholomew County Library. Gathered there on a hot evening in August 2009, a panel of five Columbus residents discussed the evening's topic, "Remembering J. Irwin Miller." The room was packed. Extra chairs were brought in. People even sat on the low carpet-covered banquettes along the walls.

Panel members were moderator Harry McCawley of the Columbus *Republic*; Owen Hungerford, Miller's longtime assistant; Tracy Souza, onetime head of the Cummins Foundation and later head of the community's Heritage Fund; Robert Stewart, former mayor; and Bob Haddad, businessman and Miller's golf buddy. After introductions, they were off—first the panel members spoke and then members of the audience who were invited to add their own comments and memories. Stories highlighted serious aspects of Miller's character and leadership, but there were also plenty of lighter anecdotes.

They remembered him as a quiet man who "didn't like to use his muscle in the community" but who nevertheless helped give the city council courage to pass the first open-housing ordinance. Thanks to his influence, they said, other civil rights legislation followed, such as an ordinance that allowed African American residents to get haircuts in Columbus rather than having to make the hour drive up to Indianapolis. They talked about his leadership in Cummins's decision to walk away from a plant in South Africa rather than conform to the hiring restrictions of apartheid.

They talked about the Irwin-Sweeney-Miller family, from whom he had inherited many of his qualities, about the four-generation Sunday dinners where he and his sister Clementine listened to discussions of the day's sermon at Tabernacle Church and current political events. (The family generally approved of President Roosevelt's financial actions during his first one hundred days, not so much his later packing of the Supreme Court.) They talked about Irwin Miller's pride in his union connections, in his honorary membership in the Diesel Workers Union, and in his negotiating philosophy: you leave a reasonable offer on the table and let the other guy say yes or no. They talked about his understanding of the impact business decisions make on people's lives and of the difficult time in the 1970s when Cummins cut back its workforce significantly. To help the affected families through the time of transition, he brought together ministers from churches in the neighboring Indiana small towns where many employees lived to a meeting at an Episcopal church in Columbus. He thought they needed to hear the economic reasons for the decisions that would affect many of the parishioners who might be turning to them for pastoral counseling.

Different speakers pulled out different actions that they thought were the most important parts of Irwin Miller's legacy. One said it was his hiring of Booz Allen Hamilton to develop a master plan to guide Cummins forward in its early days.[9] Another said it was his sending Cummins people to China, giving Cummins an early foothold in that country.[10] They talked about his love of practical jokes, his competitiveness, and his love of golf and boating, where he was reputed to be a bit of a hot rod. They talked about Miller's common touch and how he and Xenia wanted to be called by their first names (or middle name, in Irwin's case). They spoke of the beginnings of the town's architectural heritage and its unexpected, far-reaching results.

At the beginning of the evening, in a few, quick introductory words—almost an aside—moderator McCawley had said that it was time to reflect on elements of Irwin Miller's legacy, "rather than what has happened since his passing." And with much warmth, affection, and laughter, these Columbus citizens had done just that.[11]

Bartholomew County Public Library. I. M. Pei. 1969. *Carol M. Highsmith, Library of Congress*

16 Afterglow

I AM SITTING ON THE WIDE STEPS OF ARCHITECT I. M. PEI'S LOW, elegant Bartholomew County Library on Fifth Street, watching the passing scene as well as the scene being passed. It is late summer. The sun is warm. Young mothers push strollers while keeping an eye on hard-pedaling tykes on trikes. The brick plaza is perfect for this first taste of freedom for young riders—a safe, open place with Mom nearby. Spaces have to be adopted by people to be successful, as urban critic Jane Jacobs has pointed out. On the plaza between my perch and the street is sculptor Henry Moore's massive *Large Arch*, anchoring the plaza just as Pei had insisted it would. Across the street is the building that started Columbus's architectural journey, Eliel and Eero Saarinen's handsome, square, and spare First Christian Church with its tall, freestanding bell tower. To the east, just above the green treetops, I can glimpse the spire of Gunnar Birkerts's St. Peter's Lutheran Church.

Yet the aspect that makes this scene—and this town—even more unusual is the way these famous examples of modernism sit comfortably on the same street with modest midwestern frame houses with front porch swings and fancier Victorians with gingerbread trim.

Immediately to the east of where I am sitting is the massive brick Queen Anne mansion that was the home of the Irwin-Sweeney-Miller family for 134 years. Now an inn, it still conducts "a civilized conversation" with I. M. Pei's library, in the words of architect and photographer Balthazar Korab.

When Winston Churchill said, "We shape our buildings, and afterwards our buildings shape us," was he right? In what way has the unique architecture in this small American town shaped its citizens? Did Miller's idea work? Does having good architecture and public art affect the kind of people attracted to the town? Are minorities welcomed? What do children educated in Columbus's unconventional, modernist schools take away from the experience? What style houses are people building these days? Does working in a contemporary building/school all day make you want to go home to sleek granite and glass? In what style houses do the various Miller children now live—and is that relevant?

Other key aspects of Miller's vision go beyond the built environment—the importance of quality, of a diverse community citizenry, of adequate wages. According to recent figures, Bartholomew County has a median household income of $55,050, compared to $49,255 for all of Indiana. Among people twenty-five years or older, 90.3 percent have at least a high school education, a higher percent than the state and the United States as a whole.[1]

It is also important—and fair—to evaluate the results against what Miller was originally trying to accomplish. He needed to attract educated, sophisticated employees to Columbus. Those people, he surmised, would be concerned about the quality of education their children would receive in this small town. In turn, the quality of that education and the kind of teachers who could be attracted could be affected by the design and quality of the school buildings. And so it began, the grand experiment of Cummins/Miller paying architectural design fees.

The quality of managerial talent attracted to Cummins can be gauged by the health of Cummins Incorporated itself. It earned $1.39 billion on sales of $17.5 billion in 2016. It employs more than fifty-five thousand people in 190 countries and territories. For eleven years DiversityInc has named Cummins one of the Top 50 Companies for Diversity among companies with more than one thousand US-based employees, based on such areas as hiring, retaining, and promoting women, minorities, people with disabilities, LGBT employees, and veterans. It ranked twenty-first on the overall 2017 list (out of one thousand participating companies).[2] And Cummins's commitment to talent and diversity shows in its community. There is a cosmopolitan look to the families and individuals on downtown Columbus sidewalks these days.

Another important indication of the company's health is the quality of people attracted to serve on its board of directors. Franklin A. Thomas is a former president of the Ford Foundation and was a member of the Cummins board for many years. He told interviewers a few years ago that J. Irwin Miller had been "an incredible magnet for talented people who are generally interested in improving human welfare. This is true at all levels of the company." He continued, "I know that board members, without exception, have been attracted to the company because of its breadth of vision. You had the sense that when you gave your time to this company, you gave it to more than just a narrowly defined business enterprise, but also to a philosophy of business that you could feel proud of."[3]

These days Cummins markets itself as more than just a diesel engine company. In 2017 Cummins told Wall Street it was "positioned to lead in current and future technologies, including its core business [tip of the hat to Clessie Cummins and W. G. Irwin], electrification, alternative fuels and power solutions."[4] And no wonder, with Europe and the United Kingdom announcing future bans on diesel engines in new cars and vans, even if not for many decades.[5] In late summer of 2017, Cummins unveiled an electric-powered large truck at the technology center in Columbus.

A new nine-story Cummins Distribution Headquarters designed by Deborah Berke was unveiled in downtown Indianapolis in the spring of 2017. A bright red cutaway model of the workhorse QSK V16, four-stroke, sixteen-cylinder diesel engine used for drilling sits in the lobby. The building shows several important Irwin Miller influences, current Cummins chief executive officer Tom Linebarger explained during a preview open house. There's the attitude that we "ought to make the community in which we live better. . . . We do it everywhere because that's who we are." This may mean something as minor as not opening a major cafeteria within the building so that employees will go out into the community to eat lunch, supporting the historic nearby City Market and other local businesses.

Inspired by Irwin and Xenia Miller's interest in art, more than eighty pieces of framed designs, sketches, and paintings line the halls of the building. In fact, on an inner wall, stretching from the third to the eighth floors, is a colorful abstract painting inspired by a visit to the Millers' house in Columbus, according to the artist, Odili Donald Odita. The gardens "inspired awe within me."[6]

With the spacious, sleek new building in Indianapolis, an announcement of two major expenditures in Columbus by Cummins was subtle reassurance that Cummins intended to keep the company headquarters in Columbus. (Some three hundred people work in Indianapolis and eight thousand in Columbus.) One of these new expenditures concerned Cummins joining the state, county, city, and CSX Transportation in funding a $30 million railroad overpass at the west edge of downtown Columbus to ease the commute of workers to Cummins plants and offices. The second project will be a $50 million renovation of Kevin Roche's 1984 Cummins Corporate Office Building, with its verdant, vine-covered pergola.

It has been half a century, and in some cases longer, since the years of the modernist building boom in Columbus, and buildings are showing their age. "All great architecture leaks," iconoclastic architect Frank Gehry has said.[7] As if to prove his point, leaks were discovered in the skylight of the town's original architectural treasure, Eliel Saarinen's seventy-five-year-old First Christian Church. The repair goal of $160,000 was set and reached by mid-summer 2017 from the church congregation, community organizations, and individuals. The church's freestanding bell tower also needs work. "This community has a good record of taking care of things," said Richard McCoy of Landmark Columbus, one of several organizations pitching in. "I'm optimistic."[8]

North Christian Church, Eero Saarinen's church, cured its leaks with a new roof a dozen years ago. But other problems remain. Membership and attendance have fallen dramatically, resulting in diminished funds available for maintenance of this National Historic Landmark. It is one of several houses of worship working with the organization Sacred Places Indiana, affiliated with Indiana Landmarks and the national nonprofit Partners for Sacred Places. In 2018 it was also placed on Indiana Landmarks' annual 10 Most Endangered list.[9] The church's troubles are ironic given its star turn, along with the town's other Columbus modernist buildings, as spectacular backdrops in the highly praised art-house movie *Columbus*. As the film's leading characters "wander the sites, they debate such heady ideas as the healing power of buildings, modernism's relationship to religion and why—or whether—architecture means something to them," says the *New York Times* review.[10]

These days none of Irwin and Xenia Miller's children or grandchildren live in Columbus, though Will Miller and his wife, Lynn, stay involved in local institutions and projects. Much of what has made Columbus unique has been funded by Cummins and Miller family money in its many iterations: the Irwin-Sweeney-Miller Foundation (ISMF), Cummins Engine Foundation (CEF), the bank's Irwin

Union Foundation, and personal gifts from family members. But this era is drawing to a close.

With Xenia and Irwin Miller and Irwin's sister, Clementine Tangeman, all dead, an important milestone was reached in 2010. ISMF, the family foundation, announced that after several years of spending down its assets, it would henceforth dedicate the remaining assets to the Vision 20/20 project, concentrating on the enhancement of downtown Columbus at a time when Walmart and other big-box stores have left empty storefronts on so many town squares. Columbus has its own Walmart and other similar chains at the edge of town, but the town square, with its sprightly Alexander Girard–designed storefronts, does not appear to have lost its soul. In fact, one of the most historically resonant views in town is from the south side of the square, looking north from the angled front plaza of Edward Charles Bassett's 1981 Columbus City Hall. The building's lean, brick, cantilevered beams provide a perfect frame for Isaac Hodgson's 1874 Bartholomew County Courthouse across the street in Courthouse Square.

The civic torch has passed into other hands. The nonprofit organization Landmark Columbus has built on the town's art, design, and architectural heritage by organizing *Exhibit Columbus,* an annual celebration of symposiums and competitions. The pilot program for these exhibitions occurred in 2014 when designer Jonathan Nesci produced the installation "100 Variations: New Reflections on Eliel Saarinen and the Golden Ratio" in the sunken courtyard adjoining the First Christian Church. The gleaming, mirror-polished surfaces of one hundred different, small aluminum occasional tables reflected aspects of Saarinen's building and campanile. At the exhibit's opening, raindrops bounced off the tabletops, an unexpectedly appropriate touch, since the sunken area had been a reflecting pool in the church's early years.

The 2017 J. Irwin and Xenia S. Miller Prize, a juried competition, selected five designers and design teams to produce temporary installations responding to and "sparking new conversations" about iconic structures along Fifth Street in the center of town: I. M. Pei's county library with Henry Moore's *Arch* in front; Eliel Saarinen's First Christian Church across the street; Eero Saarinen's Irwin Conference Center, formerly the Irwin Union Bank headquarters; Kevin Roche's Cummins Corporate Office Building; and Mill Race Park. (The Irwin-Sweeney-Miller Foundation was one of the participating sponsors.)

For any spoilsport who grumbled that diluting Henry Moore's *Large Arch* with giant, cross-laminated timber circles was like painting a mustache on the *Mona Lisa*, one wise Columbus hand pointed out that local residents could put up with anything for three months. And it turned out that the people loved it. On the opening weekend they clambered with strollers and dogs (on leashes) up and around "Conversation Plinth," which had been inspired, said its designers, by the conversation pit in the Miller House. A dozen or so additional installations were positioned around town, including one of shimmering colors entitled "Between the Threads" by students from two Columbus high schools, several of whom are planning to study architecture and design in college. This is one of the more interesting examples of Columbus's architectural heritage—a possible career portal for students in area high schools. Indiana University in nearby Bloomington has added a Masters of Architecture degree that is based in Columbus. The program has taken over Skidmore, Owings & Merrill's glass and steel Republic building in downtown Columbus. The program is named for J. Irwin Miller.

What impact does growing up in Columbus have for kids who do not specifically see architecture or design as a career interest? "I knew that Columbus was a really special place," says Tracy Hamilton Souza, who split her growing up years between Columbus and Arlington, Virginia, after her father, Lee Hamilton, was elected to Congress. "I knew it had the attention of people who were considered important in the world of architecture, though I could not have named any architects."[11] Another youngster growing up in Columbus, Natalie Olinger-Stine, attended Harry Weese's Schmitt Elementary School and architect Norman Fletcher's Parkside Elementary, two early schools in the Cummins Foundation Architecture Program. Parkside's art teacher, Gretchen Sigmund, made sure her young pupils appreciated their surroundings and would take them outside to draw "their" building. These days the Stines proudly live in the 1953 Lauther House, one of three Harry Weese private residences in town. Natalie Stine's school experience enabled her to appreciate good architecture and influenced the family's decision to buy the house.

And then there's US vice president Mike Pence, a Columbus native who still has family living there. He was born in 1959, three years after Will Miller, the youngest of Xenia and Irwin Miller's children. The Pences were Catholic, and young Pence attended St. Columba Catholic Grade School and Northside High School, neither school yet touched by the brush of modernist architects. A 2016 headline in the *New York Times* datelined Columbus after Donald Trump picked Pence as his vice presidential running mate: "Hometown Molded Pence Even as It Began to Change." But, according to the article, the "molding" was not from exposure to world class architecture and art, but rather to conservative religious values.

Not all Columbus residents have been so enamored of Irwin Miller's leadership. One of the men in a quail hunting party in southern Indiana a few years ago was a manufacturing worker from Columbus. He complained about what he saw as Miller's heavy hand on life in Columbus. Miller, he grumbled, restricted the number of bars that could be opened in town and restricted what could be built and what could be torn down. Others complained of being forced to sell property so that projects like The Commons could be built. They were proud of what Columbus had become, but still . . .

Not surprisingly, Miller had his detractors in the rough and tumble worlds of manufacturing and corporate finance. He could be "pretty rough," said Indianapolis stockbroker William Cohrs, who sat in on meetings when young entrepreneurs presented ideas to Cummins executives.[12] "The thing I always admired about Irwin," Cummins board member Frank Thomas told another interviewer, "was his wonderful combination of a tough, competitive business drive with a complete understanding of the context within which business should operate."[13] At civic meetings Miller tended to stay in the background, and, when he did speak, he always couched his comments in diplomatic terms. "But there was an iron fist" behind those comments, noted the late newspaper columnist Harry McCawley.[14]

Recently there has been new attention, in both media and academia, to what makes a town work. Books such as *Happy City: Transforming Our Lives through Urban Design*, emphasize the importance of green space, for example. It is not "an optional luxury," writes the book's Canadian author, Charles Montgomery. "It is a crucial part of a healthy human habitat."[15] Columbus has much that is green. Settings designed by eminent landscape architects surround commercial buildings. There are hiking trails and parks, such as the eighty-five-acre Mill Race Park that winds along Flatrock River through downtown Columbus. Long ago, the Irwin-Sweeney-Miller family instinctively knew the importance of greenery to urban life. For many years the formal Italian gardens adjoining the family home on Fifth Street were open to the public at no charge for one day a week.

Irwin Miller's legacy was different things to different people. "He left a legacy of excellence," says Tracy Souza, "a legacy of community and corporate responsibility—one should be involved."[16] Even after he had officially retired from the Cummins board and withdrawn from active involvement in the community, Irwin Miller's opinions still mattered. In 2000 Cummins president Tim Solso went to Miller for advice on a new policy to offer benefits to same-sex domestic partners. Vocal opposition had developed within the company and within the town. Just before the annual meeting in April, guest opinion columns were published in Columbus's *Republic*, including pieces from Solso and former Cummins CEOs Henry Schacht, Jim Henderson—and Irwin Miller.

"Change can be difficult for any organization to accept," wrote Solso. "For some, this new policy may feel like a departure from the traditions of Cummins. In fact, just the opposite is true. This policy embodies the principles of J. Irwin Miller; principles upon which this company was founded—such as inclusion, tolerance, responsiveness and the pursuit of excellence." In his comments, Miller wrote, "This policy . . . does not judge any individual in the company but tries to see that all are treated equally and fairly. Judgment is not for us to pass but for God."[17]

To James Joseph, the former ambassador to South Africa, part of Irwin Miller's legacy has been the black alumni from Cummins who can be "found in leadership roles across a broad spectrum of American life." In addition, according to Joseph, Miller "saw the primary moral issue for business as how profits were made, rather than simply how much was given away—even for noble purposes."[18]

When people tote up all that Miller did and accomplished, "they sometimes miss that he was just a very good man," says former congressman Lee Hamilton. "He had a very broad gauged view of the world and his responsibility in it."[19]

"One of the great things about the man was, he didn't think conventionally," said former Cummins executive Jim Henderson. "He thought for himself and it was often at odds with the rest of the business community."[20] Frank Thomas met Miller when Robert Kennedy recruited businessmen to help with the redevelopment of Brooklyn's Bedford-Stuyvesant neighborhood. Thomas later became a Cummins board member and president of the Ford Foundation, with the support of Miller, who was on the Ford Foundation board. "His [Miller's] style was quite extraordinary," remembers Thomas. "Instead of projecting a dominant position, he would probe to find out what *you* thought," not necessarily about technical things but about "the broader human dimensions." For instance, Miller emphasized that "talent can reside in areas that are not obvious—you must be alert to that."[21]

In the end, what has been accomplished in Columbus can best be understood by moving beyond high school graduation rates, median income, and unemployment statistics. The truth lies in individual stories. Jonathan Nesci, the designer of the 2014 *Exhibit Columbus* pilot exhibit of one hundred aluminum tables, decided to move his family from Chicago to Columbus. "The work that my wife and I do [Christine Nesci runs an indoor spin and fitness center], we could live in any town, any city." Among the things in Columbus that appealed to the Chicago natives were the schools and the built environment. Their young sons have attended two of the schools designed with support from the Cummins Foundation: Lincoln Elementary and Central Middle School. "They can ride their bikes to school, they can ride their bikes to the pool in the summer." And up Franklin Street from Nesci's studio in the center of town is the century-old Victorian home where the family now lives. It helps that the town "is a bit of an island," not a suburb of a larger city, says Nesci. "There's much pride attached."[22]

Jill Cashen now lives in Washington, DC, where she's a union communications specialist. "I grew up in Columbus, across the street from Harry Weese's Schmitt School, learned to ride a bike in the shadow of Saarinen's First Christian Church, trained for hours in Harry Weese's Hamilton Center Ice Arena," wrote Cashen in a comment thread following a public radio program about Columbus. "My hometown is one of America's greatest treasures. It should be a lesson to all planners, architects, builders and dreamers that investing in beautiful spaces for people to grow and learn plants seeds of creativity and inspiration that last a lifetime. I hope I prove this great experiment a success by passing those seeds along to my children."[23]

NOTES

ABBREVIATIONS USED IN NOTES

JIM	J. Irwin Miller
XS, XSM	Xenia Simmons Miller
ISM	Irwin-Sweeney-Miller Family Collection at Indiana Historical Society
IHS	Indiana Historical Society, William H. Smith Memorial Library
IMA	Indianapolis Museum of Art at Newfields

1. LADY BIRD

1. Gerry LaFollette, telephone interview with author, May 22, 2013; "Lady Bird Likes Columbus, Its People," *Columbus Herald*, September 22, 1967; "Dinner Had Eclat of Capital Soiree," *Columbus Herald*, September 22, 1967; "Press Coverage Like Blanket," *The Republic* (Columbus), September 22, 1967; Jean Prather, "Lady Bird Dines in School Garden Setting," *The Republic* (Columbus), September 22, 1967.

2. "First Lady on Tour in Crossroads America," *New York Times*, September 24, 1967.

3. Ibid. Columbus's official population was 20,778 in 1960 and 26,457 in 1970 ("Columbus, Indiana Population 2019," World Population Review, accessed March 28, 2019, http://worldpopulationreview.com/us-cities/columbus-in-population).

4. "Lady Bird Likes Columbus, Its People," *Columbus Herald*, September 22, 1967.

5. The congregation changed the church's name in 1957. "First Christian Church, Columbus, Indiana: History-Heritage," 1992, archives, First Christian Church.

6. Korab, *Columbus, Indiana*, 70.

7. Spade, introduction and notes to *Eero Saarinen*, 10.

8. Henry-Russell Hitchcock and Philip Johnson, foreword to the catalog for the exhibit *Modern Architecture: International Exhibition*, February 10–March 23, 1932, Museum of Modern Art, New York, 14, 15. The catalog and exhibit evolved into a book by the same authors, *The International Style: Architecture Since 1922*.

9. Alden Whitman, "Ailene Saarinen, Art Critic Dies at 58," *New York Times*, July 15, 1972.

10. JIM to J. Henry Blessing, November 13, 1961, box 535, folder 14, ISM collection.

11. Jean Prather, "Lady Bird Dines in School Garden Setting," *The Republic* (Columbus), September 22, 1967.

12. Gerry LaFollette, "Lady Bird Toasts Columbus as 'Stone Symphony,'" *Indianapolis News*, September 22, 1967.

13. Johnson, *White House Diary*, 170.

14. "President Calls Lady Bird Here," *The Republic* (Columbus), September 22, 1967.

15. Will Miller, email to author, August 30, 2015.

16. Steven V. Roberts, "Is It Too Late for a Man of Honesty, High Purpose and Intelligence to Be Elected President of the United States in 1968?" *Esquire*, October 1967.

17. Ibid.

2. JOSEPH

1. County atlas, box 722, folder 7, ISM Collection, 107.

2. *Atlas of Bartholomew County—1879*, library reference collection, IHS, 20.

3. Box 755, folder 8, ISM Collection.

4. Pamphlet, "First Christian Church, Columbus, Indiana: History–Heritage," 2004, First Christian Church archives.

5. Terrell, *Indiana in the War of the Rebellion*, 225. Col. Terrell grew up in Bartholomew County and was onetime editor and copublisher of the *Columbus Gazette* (ibid., vii).

6. Ibid., 238.

7. Ibid., 461.

8. Pamphlet, "The Irwin Home and Gardens" (Columbus, IN: The Inn at Irwin Gardens, n.d.); Risting, *Columbus, Indiana*, 202.

9. Biographical sketch, William G. Irwin, ISM Collection, 12.

10. JIM, memoir, box 542, folder 4, ISM Collection, 20.

11. Ibid., 21.

3. MUSKOKA

1. Biographical sketch, Rev. Zachary Taylor Sweeney, ISM Collection, 9.

2. JIM to Xenia Simons, n.d. (probably early 1940s), box 463, folder 2, ISM Collection.

3. Phillips, *Indiana in Transition*, 4.

4. Biographical sketch, William G. Irwin, ISM Collection, 12.

5. Risting, *Columbus, Indiana*, 200.

6. Sweeney, *Under Ten Flags*, introductory note, iv.

7. Williams, *Stone-Campbell Movement*, 117.

8. Sweeney, *Under Ten Flags*, 396.

9. Zachary Sweeney to Linnie Sweeney, March 10, 1887, box 743, folder 4, ISM Collection.

10. *Frank Leslie's Illustrated Newspaper*, reprinted in *Christian Standard*, August 3, 1889.

11. Columbus newspapers, box 748, folders 22, 23, 24, ISM Collection.

12. "Editorial from *Indianapolis Sun*," reprinted in the *Columbus Republican*, August 16, 1900, p. 8.

4. IRWIN

1. "Irwin Funeral Here Tomorrow," *Evening Republican* (Columbus), August 15, 1910.

2. Ibid.

3. JIM, memoir (1986–1989), box 542, folder 4, ISM Collection, 22–23.

4. Ibid., 25.

5. Ibid., 24–28.

6. Biographical sketch, Hugh Th. Miller, box 755, folder 8, ISM Collection, 11.

7. *Thirty-Fourth Annual Report of the Indiana State Board of Health*, 1915 (Fort Wayne, IN: Fort Wayne Printing Company, 1917), accessed April 11, 2019, https://archive.org/details/88unkngoog/page/n5, 168, 170, 181. Though contagious, "pulmonary consumption" was not among diseases for which people were quarantined (Rule 10, 139).

8. Irwin Mss. (W. G. Irwin and Hugh Th. Miller Papers), IU Lilly Library, Bloomington.

9. JIM, memoir, 6.

10. Ibid., 4.

11. Ibid., 6.

12. Ibid., 4–6, 15. Ibid.

13. Ibid., 29.

14. Ibid., 30–32.

15. Ibid., 5.

16. Roberts, "Is It Too Late," *Esquire*, October 1967: 89–93, 173, 175, 178, 180–84.

17. *The Annual*, 1927, 72 (Taft School archives).

18. *The Oracle*, February 1927, 20–21. Mack, Miller's roommate at Yale, would become a renowned Shakespearian scholar and beloved professor at Yale and a lifelong friend of the Miller family.

19. JIM to W. G. Irwin, n.d., box 459, folder 17, ISM Collection. Ibid.

20. Kelley, *Yale: A History*, 387.

21. T. George Harris, "Egghead in the Diesel Industry," *Fortune*, October 1957, 258.

22. Ibid, citing Pierson, *Yale*.

23. Pierson, *Yale*, vol. 2, 108.

24. Suzanne Noruschat, Yale Manuscripts and Archives, email to author, March 4, 2016.

25. C. H. Sawyer, Obituary of Everett Victor Meeks 1879–1954, in *College Art Journal*, 1955, issue 3, 295.

26. Merkel, *Eero Saarinen*, 242.

27. Harris, "Egghead in the Diesel Industry," 262.

28. James W. Hoffman, "J. Irwin Miller, Churchman and Industrialist," *Presbyterian Life*, February 15, 1962.

29. Ibid.

30. Elizabeth Nie, "Different by Design," Indianapolis Woman's Club, box 18, folder 5, Collection M0478, IHS.

31. Gemmecke, "W. G. Irwin and Hugh Thomas Miller," 333; Blum, *Oral History*, 81,

32. Gemmecke, "W. G. Irwin and Hugh Thomas Miller," 294.

33. Ibid., 294, note 36.

5. CLESSIE

1. L. Cummins, *Diesel Odyssey*, 25–26, quoting his father's book, *My Days with the Diesel.*

2. Curtis Redgap, "Clessie Lyle Cummins and Cummins Diesel Engines," accessed September 6, 2017, http://www.allpar.com/corporate/bios/cummins.html.

3. Gemmecke, "W. G. Irwin and Hugh Thomas Miller," 209–10.

4. "The First Super Speedway," A Mark Dill Enterprises Inc. Website, accessed June 17, 2013, http://www.firstsuperspeedway.com/articles/indiana-auto-manufacturers-1909, quoting the *Indianapolis Star*, August 15, 1909, special edition at the time of the first race at the Indianapolis Motor Speedway (though not a five-hundred-mile race).

5. L. Cummins, *Diesel Odyssey*, 52.

6. Ibid., 34.

7. Ibid., 35.

8. Ibid., 40.

9. Ibid., 103–4.

10. Ibid., 53, 55–56.

11. Ibid., 56.

12. The part of the old Cerealine building that housed the original mill became Cummins Machine Works and later Cummins Engine Company before it was torn down in 1950. The rest of the four-story building was restored in 1980.

13. The patent was for Germany, Switzerland, the United Kingdom, and the United States.

14. Gemmecke, "W. G. Irwin and Hugh Thomas Miller," 196–200.

15. "Fuel Conversion Factors to Gasoline Gallon Equivalents," State & Alternative Fuel Provider Fleets/compliance, https://epact.energy.gov/fuel-conversion-factors; D. David Kriplen, BSME, PE, interview with author.

16. L. Cummins, *Diesel Odyssy*, 57.

17. "Articles of Incorporation of Cummins Engine Company," January 31 and February 3, 1919, "Minutes of First Meeting of Directors," February 21, 1919, Cummins Archives; Cummins, *Diesel Odyssey*, 58.

18. L. Cummins, *Diesel Odyssey*, 78.

19. C. Cummins, *My Days with the Diesel*, 182.

20. Gemmecke, "W. G. Irwin and Hugh Thomas Miller," 225, note 34.

21. L. Cummins, *Diesel Odyssey*, 144.

22. Ibid., 196–98.

23. Ibid., 203.

24. Elizabeth Nie, "Sage," Indianapolis Woman's Club, March 19, 2004, based on research in the Elizabeth Sage Historic Costume Collection, Indiana University, box 18, folder 5, collection M0478, IHS.

25. L. Cummins, *Diesel Odyssey*, 205.

26. Ibid., 297.

27. Irwin Bank merged with the Union Trust Company in 1928 (Gemmecke, *W. G. Irwin*, 21, 22, note 47).

28. Gemmecke, "W. G. Irwin and Hugh Thomas Miller," 296, citing W. G. Irwin to Linnie Sweeney, July 3, 1933.

6. ELIEL AND EERO

1. "First Christian Church, Columbus, Indiana, History–Heritage," pamphlet, 2004, First Christian Church archive. The congregation would change the name again from Tabernacle Church of Christ to First Christian Church in 1957.

2. Elsie Irwin Sweeney, "Symbolism of the First Christian Church," typescript, First Christian Church archive, Columbus, n.d., 1.

3. Ibid.

4. Ibid.

5. Spade, introduction and notes, *Eero Saarinen*, 11.

6. Peter, *Oral History of Modern Architecture*, 193.

7. Spade, *Eero Saarinen*, 11.

8. Temko, *Eero Saarinen*, 16.

9. "Piety in Brick," *Time*, January 27, 1941.

10. Sweeney, "Symbolism," 2.

11. Brooks, "Miller House," 12; Sweeney, "Symbolism," 2.

12. "Celebrating 150 Years of God's Faithfulness at First Christian Church," 2005, First Christian Church archive.

13. "Our History & Heritage," pamphlet, First Christian Church archive.

14. "Piety in Brick," *Time*, January 27, 1941.

15. Sweeney, "Symbolism," 3.

16. "1,500 Present at Laying of Cornerstone," *The Republic* (Columbus), April 21, 1941.

17. Temko, *Eero Saarinen*, 16.

18. Thiry, Bennett, and Kamphoefner, *Churches & Temples*, 58.

7. XENIA

1. XSM, memoir, box 585, folder 9, ISM Collection.

2. JIM to W. G. Irwin, April 4, 1936, as quoted in Gemmecke, "W. G. Irwin and Hugh Thomas Miller," 297.

3. Gemmecke, "W. G. Irwin and Hugh Thomas Miller," 290, referencing data mentioned in "Diesels on Wheels," *Fortune*, December 1934, 106–16, 119–20. Data cited appears on pp. 106, 116.

4. Unpublished memo "Profit and Surplus History," n.d., quoted in Gemmecke, "W. G. Irwin and Hugh Thomas Miller," 290.

5. Cummins, *Diesel Odyssey*, 252.

6. "Cummins People Vote to Negotiate Direct with Firm," *Republican* (Columbus), May 22, 1937, quoted in L. Cummins, *Diesel Odyssey*, 252.

7. T. George Harris, "Egghead in the Diesel Industry," *Fortune*, October 1957, 264.

8. XSM, memoir, box 585, folder 9, ISM Collection, 3.

9. JIM to XS, July 17, box 463, folder 2. ISM Collection.

10. JIM to XS, June 7, 1942, box 463, folder 2, ISM Collection.

11. JIM to XS, box 463, folder 1, ISM Collection.

12. XS to JIM, box 463, folder 1, ISM Collection.

13. L. Cummins, *Diesel Odyssey*, 287–88; "Diesel-Powered Tank Is Sent to Proving Ground," *Republic* (Columbus), October 20, 1941.

14. JIM to XS, box 463, folder 2, ISM Collection.

15. Ibid.

16. L. Cummins, *Diesel Odyssey*, 296.

17. JIM, journal, box 542, folder 4, ISM Collection, 4.

18. L. Cummins, *Diesel Odyssey*, 296.

19. An entity called Oil Engine Development Company (OEDC) had been organized in 1922 with 50 percent of the stock to Cummins, 49

percent to W. G. Irwin, and 1 percent to Linnie Sweeney. OEDC merged with Cummins Engine Company in 1941–42. See Gemmecke, "W. G. Irwin and Hugh Thomas Miller," 226–229, 311; L. Cummins, *Diesel Odyssey,* 292–95, 322.

20. $2.25 million figure from memo, JIM to W. G. Irwin, April 4, 1936, quoted by Gemmecke, "W. G. Irwin and Hugh Thomas Miller," 297.

21. Gemmecke, "W. G. Irwin and Hugh Thomas Miller," 303, n. 58.

22. L. Cummins, *Diesel Odyssey,* 294.

8. HOME

1. *Dictionary of American Naval Fighting Ships,* vol. IV (1969), 47–48, http://www.history.navy.mil/danfs/13/langley-ii.htm.

2. Ibid.

3. T. George Harris, "Egghead in the Diesel Industry," *Fortune,* Oct.1957.

4. James W. Hoffman, "J. Irwin Miller, Churchman and Industrialist," *Presbyterian Life,* Feb. 15, 1962.

5. "Robert Tangeman of Seminary Dies," *New York Times,* September 27, 1964.

6. "A Study in Small-Town Progress," *Architectural Forum,* October 1955, 161–64.

7. Will Miller, "Eero and Irwin: Praiseworthy Competition with One's Ancestors, " in *Eero Saarinen: Shaping the Future,* 61.

8. The bank building is now the Irwin Conference Center.

9. John Peter, *The Oral History of Modern Architecture,* typed transcript, box 7, folder 74, 40–41, Recorded Sound Reference Center, Library of Congress.

10. Marvin Mass, *The Invisible Architect,* 67.

11. Bradley Brooks, *Miller House and Garden,* 14.

12. Alexandra Lange, lecture at Columbus Visitors' Center, June 23, 2016.

13. Brooks, *Miller House,* 16. As a decorating trend, conversation pits proved to be impractical and generally did not catch on.

14. Kevin Roche to author. Roche was not particularly a fan of the idea.

15. Frank Wilking to JIM, May 11, 1956, Miller House archives, Indianapolis Museum of Art, IMA Archives Portal, archive.imauseum.org; *Indianapolis Star,* November 19, 2008.

16. Suzanne Stephens, critic and author, Miller House Symposium, May 20, 2011, at the Indianapolis Museum of Art. Stephens listed the other four as the Philip Johnson Glass House, New Canaan, Connecticut, (Johnson, 1940); Eames House and the Entenza House next door, Pacific Palisades, California, (Eero Saarinen and Charles Eames, 1949); Farnsworth House, Plano, Illinois (Mies Van der Rohe, 1951).

9. HARRY

1. Blum, *Oral History*, 209.
2. Bruegmann, *Architecture of Harry Weese*, 37.
3. JIM to Harry Weese, October 11, 1950, Columbus Architectural Archives.
4. Harry Weese to Eero Saarinen, October 17, 1950, Columbus Architectural Archives.
5. Blum, "Oral History," 209.
6. Risting, *Columbus, Indiana*, 215.
7. T. Kelly Wilson, "Harry Weese Creative Syncretism," IUCA+D, Columbus, April 4–5, 2014, 35.
8. Korab, *Columbus, Indiana*, 82.
9. Bruegmann, *Architecture of Harry Weese*, 37.
10. Tragically, alcoholism destroyed Weese and his career and ruined his chance to oversee the additions to his earlier Columbus buildings. He died nearly forgotten in a Manteno, Illinois, veterans' home in 1998 (Ian Baldwin, "The Architecture of Harry Weese," *Places Journal*, May 2011; Robert Sharoff, "On the Life and Work of Chicago Architect Harry Weese," *Chicago Magazine*, July 2012; Herbert Muschamp, obituary, *New York Times*, November 3, 1998.)
11. Through the years, the lists of architects have never been made public.
12. ISM Collection, box 535, folder 14, IHS.
13. Margaret Miller, interview with author, June 4, 2015.
14. Risting, *Columbus, Indiana*, 48–49.
15. Bruegmann, *Architecture of Harry Weese*, 111–13; author visit, August 2015.
16. *Fortune* 500 archive, http://archive.fortune.com/magazines/fortune/fortune500_archive/full/1955/401.html.

17. Richard D. N. Dickinson, essay "J. Irwin Miller: Industrialist, Ecumenist, Community Leader," typescript, archives, Christian Theological Seminary, 2.

18. Risting, *Columbus, Indiana*, 46.

19. Watkins, *Christian Theological Seminary, Indianapolis*, 143.

20. Ibid., 95.

21. Ibid., 147.

22. Ibid., 149.

23. Reminiscences of Eugene Carson Blake, oral history, [198?], 29–30, Henry Knox Sherrill Project, Center for Oral History, Columbia University Libraries, History Collection.

24. Ibid., 30–31.

10. JFK, LBJ, JIM

1. Findlay, *Church People*, 48.

2. Findlay, *Church People*, 33.

3. Branch, *Parting the Waters*, 833–34. King, Roy Wilkens, and other black leaders did have a meeting with Kennedy five days later.

4. Louis F. Oberdorfer, assistant attorney general, memorandum to JIM, June 20, 1963, box 023, Lee White Papers, JFK Presidential Library and Museum.

5. JIM to Louis F. Oberdorfer, June 21, 1963.

6. Fay Williams, interview with author, December 7, 2016.

7. Lewis, Aydin, and Powell, *March: Book Two*, 168.

8. Findlay, *Church People*, 50.

9. Margaret Miller, interview with author, June 4, 2015; Owen Hungerford, email to author, November 21, 2013.

10. National Council of Churches, press release September 19, 1963, box 1, folder 1, ISM Collection.

11. Ibid.

12. Findlay, *Church People*, 55.

13. Risen, *Bill of the Century*, 149, 175, 237.

14. Risen, *Bill of the Century*, 5, quoting *Richard B. Russell, Jr.* by Gilbert C. Fite, University of Georgia professor and Russell biographer.

15. Risen, *Bill of the Century*, 3.

16. National Park Service, "Civil Rights Act of 1964," accessed December 3, 2016, www.nps.gov/subjects/civilrights/1964-civil-rights-act.htm.

17. Memo from G. L. Robillard, J. I. Miller's administrative assistant, box 301, folder 1, ISM Collection.

18. S. E. Lauther to G. L. Robillard, Sept. 23, 1963, box 301, folder 1, ISM Collection.

19. H. J. Fiers, "Negro Employment Report," September 16, 1963, box 301, folder 1, ISM Collection.

20. H. W. Abts to G. L. Robillard, September 24, 1963, box 301, folder 1, ISM Collection.

21. Claudia Stevens Maddox, interviews with author, n.d.

22. George Ade, "Indiana" in *Single Blessedness, and Other Observations* (Garden City, NY: Doubleday, Page and Company, 1922).

23. S. E. Lauther to G. L. Robillard, September 23, 1963, box 301, folder 1, ISM Collection.

24. Jim Joseph, telephone interview with author, August 1, 2017.

25. JIM speech, "Urban Problems Affect Us All," February 6, 1968, box 530, folder 14, ISM Collection.

26. Maddox, interviews with author, n.d.

27. Minutes, Common Council Meeting of the City of Columbus, January 6, 1969.

28. Cruikshank and Sicilia, *Engine That Could*, 238, quoting JIM to Mayor Eret Kline, December 10, 1968; Joseph, *Saved for a Purpose*, 99; Minutes, Columbus Common Council Meeting, January 20, 1969.

29. Cruikshank and Sicilia, *Engine That Could*, 322–23.

30. Joseph, telephone interview with author, August 1, 2017.

31. Cruikshank and Sicilia, *Engine That Could*, 325, citing *Iron Age*, "Companies Must Be Good Citizens," August 23, 1976.

32. Jim Joseph to *The Republic*, as quoted in "News from the National Council of Churches," obituary of J. Irwin Miller, August 18, 2004. No specific occasion has been pinpointed at which King made this statement. Jim Joseph believes it first became widely known through Andrew Young, civil rights friend and associate of Martin Luther King Jr.

11. FAREWELLS

1. Yale University Library, Corporation Fellows, Successors to Founding Trustees.

2. Kabaservice, *Guardians*, 220.

3. Ibid.

4. Kabaservice, *Guardians*, 220, quoting Irwin Miller to John McKay Jr., October 2, 1964, Brewster Presidential Records RU II I-126:15, Yale University.

5. Kabaservice, *Guardians*, 220.

6. Ibid., 237.

7. Kingman Brewster Memorial Service, box 543, folder 14, ISM Collection.

8. David Goodrich, Henry Schacht, Jim Henderson, Lee Hamilton, interviews with author. After sixteen months Goodrich left to go to graduate school, with the blessing of the Miller organization. He would return many years later as a member of the board of directors of Irwin Union Bank. Schacht and Henderson both served later as Cummins CEOs. Hamilton was elected to Congress from Indiana's Ninth District, where he served thirty-four years.

9. Curtis Redgap, "Clessie Lyle Cummins and Cummins Diesel Engines," Allpar.com, 2008, http://www.allpar.com/corporate/bios/cummins.html.

10. Cruikshank and Sicilia, *Engine That Could*, 138.

11. Ibid., 138–39.

12. L. Cummins, *Diesel Odyssey*, 362.

13. Ibid.

14. Cruikshank and Sicilia, *Engine That Could*, 169–70.

15. L. Cummins, *Diesel Odyssey*, 314, 332, 346 note 28.

16. Ibid., 342.

17. Ibid., 387–88.

18. *Cummins Management Newsletter*, September 27, 1968, as quoted in *Engine That Could*, 242.

19. Cruikshank and Sicilia, *Engine That Could*, 168.

12. THE KISS

1. Risting, *Columbus, Indiana*, 170.

2. Henry Moore to JIM, June 16, 1970, box 555, folder 12, ISM Collection.

3. JIM to Moore, April 20, 1971, box 555, folder 12, ISM Collection.

4. Lee Hamilton to JIM, May 3, 1971, box 555, folder 12, ISM Collection.

5. John Russell, "Henry Moore, Sculptor of an Age, Dies at 88," *New York Times*, September 1, 1986.

6. Lee Hamilton, interview with author, November 19, 2014.

7. Risting, *Columbus, Indiana*, 68.

8. Quotes from Lady Bird Johnson's diary here and below are from Lady Bird Johnson, social diary, November 14, 1967, 1, 10, 12–13, White House Social Entertainment File, LBJ Library.

9. Libby and Jim Rowe were longtime Washington friends of the Johnsons and had a daughter, Elizabeth (Elspeth). Libby Rowe, a Kennedy appointee to the national Capital Planning Commission, advised Lady Bird on her beautification efforts.

10. Marilyn Wellemeyer, "An Inspired Renaissance in Indiana," *Life*, November 17, 1967, 74.

11. Caroli, *Lady Bird and Lyndon*, 323.

12. Mrs. J. Irwin Miller to Mrs. Lyndon Johnson, November 18, 1967, social files, LBJ Library.

13. JIM to Mrs. Lyndon Johnson, November 18, 1967, social files LBJ Library.

14. Claudia Stevens Maddox, interviews with author, n.d.

15. Biographical Sketch, Joseph Irwin Miller, at the beginning of the ISM Collection index.

16. Lee Hamilton, interview with author, November 19, 1914.

17. Reminiscences of Alan Pifer and Eli Evans, Oral History, 1970, Carnegie Corporation Project, Columbia Center for Oral History, Columbia University Libraries.

18. *Link*, Christian Theological Seminary, spring 2009, 20–21.

19. Will Miller, interview with author, May 1, 2015.

20. "Multimillion Dollar Castalia Mansion in Columbus Set for Auction," *The Republic*, October 8, 2008; Tricia Gilson, Columbus Architectural Archives; Beth Lowe, email to author.

21. Details of this takeover drama are from Cruikshank and Sicilia, *Engine That Could*, 413–17, in a chapter aptly titled "Circling the Wagons."

13. MANDELA

1. Wayne Fredericks to JIM, August 18, 1993, box 395, folder 6, ISM Collection.

2. Bill Keller, "Nelson Mandela, South Africa's Liberator as Prisoner and President, Dies at 95," *New York Times*, December 5, 2013.

3. JIM to Henry Schacht, September 30, 1993, box 395, folders 5,6, ISM Collection.

4. Henry Schacht, interview with author, May 3, 2017.

5. JIM to Chief Justice M. M. Corbett, April 28, 1994, box 395, folder 6, ISM Collection.

6. "The Pritzker Architectural Prize, Christian de Portzamparc 1994," official program, Los Angeles: Jensen & Walker, Inc., Jury Citation, 3.

7. Ibid., 12.

8. Ibid., 39.

9. Ibid., Bill Lacy, secretary to [Pritzker] jury, 14–15.

10. Kevin Roche, email to author, May 18, 2016.

11. Ibid.

14. BACH

1. Will Miller, interview with author, May 1, 2015.

2. Kabaservice, *Guardians*, 220.

3. JIM to Will Miller, November 21, 1998, box 482, folder 4, ISM Collection.

4. Cho-Liang Lin, telephone interview with author, January 10, 2018.

5. Tom Beczkiewicz, interview with author, February 16, 2014.

6. Ibid.

7. Charles Webb to Charles Rentschler, oral interview recordings, DVD 310–11, ISM Collection.

8. This is the violin that Lin plays today. The family's other Strad, the 1708 Swaal, was sold to a professor on the East Coast. The Guarneri del Gesu went to Europe. Lin says he would have been happy with any one of the three.

9. Henry Schacht, interview with author, May 5, 2017.

10. Memo, box 484, folder 6, ISM Collection.

11. Brian Blair, "Miller Recalled Fondly at Visitation," *The Republic* (Columbus), August 19, 2004, 1.

12. JIM to Will Miller, November 28, 1998, box 482, folder 4, ISM Collection.

13. Ibid.

14. Memorial service program, box 485, folder 2, ISM Collection.

15. John Young, Windermere, box 484 folder 6, ISM Collection.

15. AKA POP

1. Kathleen McLaughlin, "Miller Brothers Who Shared in Fortune Fighting Over $3 Million," *Indianapolis Business Journal*, June 5, 2010, quoting July 5, 1996, letter. Additional background in Indiana Court of Appeals, No. 03A01–0912-CV-586, September 30, 2010.

2. McLaughlin, "Miller Brothers," quoting 1991 and 1992 letters, *Indianapolis Business Journal*, June 5, 2010.

3. McLaughlin, "Miller Brothers," *Indianapolis Business Journal*, June 5, 2010.

4. Ibid.

5. Ibid.

6. Henry Schacht, interview with author, May 3, 2017.

7. David Goodrich, interview with author, October 22, 2015.

8. Jeff Swiatek, "Irwin's Rich History in Banking Ends," *Indianapolis Star*, September 19, 2009, 1.

9. Panel member Owen Hungerford.

10. Charlie Rentschler, who, after leaving Cummins, wrote a biography of J. Irwin Miller, *The Cathedral Builder*, published in 2014. His interviews and extensive research in the Irwin-Sweeney-Miller Collection at the Indiana Historical Society were helpful to the author of this book.

11. Newspaperman and Columbus historian Harry McCawley died in September 2017 as this book was being completed.

16. AFTERGLOW

1. QuickFacts table, United States Census Bureau, accessed August 21, 2017, 2016 figures, https://www.census.gov/quickfacts/fact/table/US/PSTO45216.

2. Cummins news release, *Business Wire*, June 27, 2017.

3. Cruikshank and Sicilia, *Engine That Could*, 515.

4. Cummins press release, June 15, 2017.

5. "Britain to Ban New Diesel and Gas Cars by 2040," *New York Times*, July 26, 2017.

6. Odili Donald Odita, "The Wisdom of Trees," informational wall plaque, Cummins Indianapolis Distribution Headquarters.

7. Michael Blackwood's film, *Frank Gehry*, as quoted in Naomi Miller's review in *Progressive Architecture*, June 1989, 130.

8. Patrick Sisson, "Restoring Eero and Eliel Saarinen's First Christian Church, A Modernist Icon in Columbus," *Curbed*, February 2, 2017.

9. "10 Most Endangered," Indiana Landmarks, accessed March 25, 2019, https://www.indianalandmarks.org/10-most-endangered.

10. Ben Kenigsberg, "Modernism's Promise and an Auspicious Feature Debut in 'Columbus,'" *New York Times*, August 3, 2017.

11. Tracy Souza, telephone interview with author, August 3, 2017.

12. William Cohrs, telephone interview with author, February 17, 2014.

13. Cruikshank and Sicilia, *Engine That Could*, 515.

14. Harry McCawley, interview with author, n.d.

15. Montgomery, *Happy City*, 120.

16. Tracy Souza, telephone interview with author, August 3, 2017.

17. Hanafee, *Red, Black and Global*, 77–82.

18. Joseph, *Saved for a Purpose*, 100, 105.

19. Lee Hamilton, interview with author, November 19, 2014.

20. Jim Henderson, interview with author, February 2, 2016.

21. Frank Thomas, telephone interview with author, May 10, 2017.

22. Jonathan Nesci, telephone interview with author, December 11, 2017.

23. Susan Stamberg, National Public Radio, July 31, 2012; Jill Cashen, email to author, August 30, 2017.

BIBLIOGRAPHY

GENERAL

Ade, George. "Indiana." In *Single Blessedness, and Other Observations*, 172–77.

Branch, Taylor. *Parting the Waters: America in the King Years, 1954–63*. New York: Simon & Schuster, 1988.

Brown, John T. *Churches of Christ*. Louisville, KY: John P. Morton & Co., 1904.

Caroli, Betty Boyd. *Lady Bird and Lyndon: The Hidden Story of a Marriage That Made a President*. New York: Simon & Schuster, 2015.

Cruikshank, Jeffrey L., and David B. Sicilia. *The Engine That Could: Seventy-Five Years of Values-Driven Change at Cummins Engine Company*. Boston, MA: Harvard Business School Press, 1997.

Cummins, Clessie. *My Days with the Diesel: The Memoirs of Clessie L. Cummins, Father of the Highway Diesel*. Philadelphia, PA: Chilton Books, ca. 1967.

Cummins, Lyle. *The Diesel Odyssey of Clessie Cummins*. Columbus, IN: Cummins, 2012.

Findlay, James F., Jr. *Church People in the Struggle: The National Council of Churches and the Black Freedom Movement, 1950–1970*. New York: Oxford University Press, 1993.

Gemmecke, Richard H. "W. G. Irwin and Hugh Thomas Miller: A Study in Free Enterprise in Indiana." PhD diss., Department of History, Indiana University: 1955. (Gemmecke used Irwin Estate General Files, letters of W. G. Irwin 1904–1947, microfilm, 102 reels.)

Hanafee, Susan. *Red, Black and Global: The Transformation of Cummins 1995–2010*. Columbus, IN: Cummins, 2011.

Jacobs, Jane. *The Death and Life of Great American Cities*. New York: Modern Library, Fiftieth Anniversary Edition, 2011. Originally published by Random House, 1961.

Johnson, Lady Bird. *A White House Diary*. Austin, TX: LBJ Presidential Library, 1970.

Joseph, James A. *Saved for a Purpose: A Journey from Private Virtues to Public Values*. Durham, NC: Duke University Press, 2015.

Kabaservice, Geoffrey. *The Guardians: Kingman Brewster, His Circle, and the Rise of the Liberal Establishment*. New York: H. Holt and Co., 2004.

Kanigel, Robert. *Eyes on the Street: The Life of Jane Jacobs*. New York: Alfred A. Knopf, 2016.

Kelley, Brooks Mather. *Yale: A History*. New Haven, CT: Yale University Press, 1974.

Lewis, John, Andrew Aydin, and Nate Powell. *March: Book Two*. Marietta, GA: Top Shelf Productions, 2015.

Merrell, James L. "J. Irwin Miller." Chap. 9 in *They Live Their Faith; Portraits of Men and Women with a Mission*. St. Louis, MO: Bethany Press, 1965.

Montgomery, Charles. *Happy City: Transforming Our Lives through Urban Design*. New York: Farrar, Straus and Giroux, 2013.

Pierson, George Wilson. *Yale: College and University, vol. 2, 1921–1937*. New Haven, CT: Yale University Press, 1960.

Phillips, Clifton J. *Indiana in Transition: The Emergence of an Industrial Commonwealth 1880–1920*. Indianapolis: Indiana Historical Bureau and Indiana Historical Society, 1968.

Risen, Clay. *The Bill of the Century: The Epic Battle for the Civil Rights Act*. New York: Bloomsbury Press, 2014.

Rentschler, Charles E. Mitchell. *The Cathedral Builder: A Biography of J. Irwin Miller*. Bloomington, IN: Author House, 2014.

Sweeney, Z. T. *Under Ten Flags*. Cincinnati, OH: Standard Publishing Co., 1888.

Terrell, W. H. H. *Indiana in the War of the Rebellion: Report of the Adjutant General*. Indianapolis: Indiana Historical Bureau, 1869; reprint 1960.

Watkins, Keith. *Christian Theological Seminary, Indianapolis: A History of Education for Ministry*. Indianapolis: Guild Press of Indiana, 2001.

Williams, D. Newell. *The Stone-Campbell Movement: A Global History*. St. Louis, MO: Chalice Press, 2012.

ARCHITECTURE

Blum, Betty J., *Oral History of Harry Mohr Weese*. Chicago: Art Institute of Chicago, 1991, 2001.

Brooks, Bradley C. *Miller House and Garden*. New York: Assouline, 2011.

Bruegmann, Robert, *The Architecture of Harry Weese*. New York: W. W. Norton, 2010.

Goldberger, Paul, *Why Architecture Matters*. New Haven, CT, and London: Yale University Press, 2009.

Hitchcock, Henry-Russell, and Philip Johnson. *The International Style: Architecture Since 1922*. 1st ed. New York: W. W. Norton, 1932; reprinted 1997.

Hitchcock, Henry-Russell, and Philip Johnson. *Modern Architecture: International Exhibition*. February 10–March 23, 1932. Museum of Modern Art, New York.

Korab, Balthazar, *Columbus, Indiana: An American Landmark*. Kalamazoo, MI: Documan Press, 1989.

Lange, Alexandra, *Mastering the Language of Buildings and Cities*. New York: Princeton Architectural Press, 2012.

Mass, Marvin, with Janet Adams Strong. *The Invisible Architect*. New York: Piloti Press, 2012.

Merkel, Jayne. *Eero Saarinen*. London: Phaidon Press, 2014.

Miller, Will. "Eero and Irwin: Praiseworthy Competition with One's Ancestors." In *Eero Saarinen: Shaping the Future*, edited by Eeva-Liisa Pelkonen and Donald Albrecht, 57–67. New Haven, CT: Yale University Press, 2006.

Peter, John. *The Oral History of Modern Architecture: Interviews with the Greatest Architects of the Twentieth Century*. New York: H. N. Abrams, 1994.

Risting, Steven R. *Columbus, Indiana: A Look at Modern Architecture & Art*. Columbus, IN: Columbus Area Visitors Center, 2012.

Ramirez, Enrique, Amy Auscherman, and Matt Shaw. *Didactic III: Collection on Exhibit Columbus*. Indianapolis: PRINTtEXT, 2016.

Spade, Rupert, *Eero Saarinen*. New York: Simon & Schuster, 1971.

Thiry, Paul, Richard Bennett, and H. L. Kamphoefner. *Churches & Temples*. New York: Reinhold, 1954.

Temko, Allan. *Eero Saarinen*. New York: G. Braziller, 1962.

INDEX

Note: Page numbers in *italics* indicate photographs.

NANCY KRIPLEN is author of two previous biographies, *Dwight Davis: The Man and the Cup* and *The Eccentric Billionaire: John D. MacArthur—Empire Builder, Reluctant Philanthropist, Relentless Adversary*. She has worked on the editorial staffs of *Time* magazine and Scripps-Howard's *Indianapolis Times*, and her freelance articles have appeared in the *New York Times, Smithsonian, Bloomberg.com, Discover*, and other publications.

ACQUISITIONS EDITOR	Ashley Runyon
PROJECT MANAGER	Nancy Lightfoot
BOOK AND COVER DESIGNER	Pamela Albert Rude
COMPOSITION COORDINATOR	Tony Brewer